By

J. Christine Catalani
and
Cathleen McAuliffe

Illustrated by
Olivia Cole
and
Doris Simone

Fearon Teacher Aids

Editor: Suzanne Moyers

FEARON TEACHER AIDS
An Imprint of Modern Curriculum
A Division of Simon & Schuster
299 Jefferson Road, P.O. Box 480
Parsippany, NJ 07054-0480

 ISBN 1-56417-858-7

1 2 3 4 5 6 7 8 9 TCS 01 00 99 98 97 96

CONTENTS

INTRODUCTION

NURTURING THE WHOLE CHILD

As a teacher of young children, you play an important role in the development of the whole child. You teach not only physical, cognitive, and language skills, but social and emotional skills, as well. The way you set up your room and interact with each child may influence a student for years to come.

Think of the goals you have for your students. Chances are, helping them become independent, confident learners ranks high on the list. The approach we describe in *Let the Kids Do It!* frees you from spending a disproportionate amount of time managing behavior, so that you can spend more time developing creative lessons and teaching children one-on-one.

One way to do that is by using rebus cues, signs that explain, for instance, how to put blocks away, the number of children that belong in a center at one time, or where to throw away a tissue. As they follow the signs, children will begin to take more responsibility for their learning, becoming more involved in decision making and controlling their own behavior in the process. Sample rebus charts, as well as other kinds of pictorial signs, are included at the end of many chapters throughout this book.

MORE SUGGESTIONS IN THIS BOOK

Besides using rebus cues, other suggestions in this book include:

- new ideas for planning curriculum
- ways to organize the room
- scheduling tips
- effective use of transitional activities
- establishing routines and limits

As you read, you'll think of ways to adapt these ideas to your own classroom, but you can start right away by asking yourself where you spend the most time giving directions and reminders or helping children use materials constructively. Do children seem to have plenty of ideas for using materials? Are they putting the materials back in place after playing with them? Are children avoiding a particular area or becoming involved in too many conflicts during certain activities? If the answer to any of these questions is *no*, the tips in this book are especially for you.

Contrast these two classrooms:

The children in this room are dependent on the teacher for all directions. Children frequently spend time just waiting for those directions. The teacher feels as though everyone needs something from her. He feels more like a police officer than a teacher.

This teacher carefully introduced these children to the room, routines, and schedule. Children learned that there are other sources of information besides the teacher. Cues remind them where to put materials. Rebuses offer ideas for using learning center materials.

Chapter Checklist

Use this checklist to evaluate your room. For any *no* response, refer to the chapter for suggestions.

Are the children in the class	**Yes**	**No**	**Chapter(s)**
... showing familiarity with routines and schedule?			6, 7
... moving from center to center without direct assistance?			8, 9
... making choices and decisions about activities in centers?			1, 2, 5
... cleaning up and putting away materials?			7
... learning to solve problems by themselves?			8
Do you and other adults have time to			
... model caring behaviors toward children and other adults?			8
... listen to children?			1
... observe children's progress or assist them in thinking through tasks?			3, 5
... assist children in developing problem-solving skills?			8
... adequately plan activities to expand on children's skills?			1

Terminology note: infants = birth to one year; young toddlers = approx. one to 2 1/2 years; older toddlers = about 2 1/2 to three years; preschoolers = about three to five years.

1

Interest Centers in Classroom Arrangement

Good room arrangement and the proper location of supplies and materials stimulate indirect learning and self-directed behavior. When materials are accompanied by effective cues, children learn to put things in their places as they practice organizational skills.

Survey Your Space

Before arranging (or rearranging) your room, consider the following:

- location of exits and entrances
- traffic flow or patterns of movement
- location of water and electrical outlets
- location and availability of storage places for toys and other teaching materials
- sources of natural and artificial light
- locations of restrooms and kitchen
- spaces for eating and sleeping
- storage and cubbies
- floor coverings
- general appearance of the room
- interconnection between areas

1 Draw the Room to Scale

Draw your room to scale on graph paper. Indicate immovable features like tiled and carpeted floors, restrooms, doors, and windows.

2 Divide the Room into Age-Specific Areas

Toddlers and preschoolers require different developmental approaches. You'll want your room set-up to reflect these different needs.

Toddler Rooms Divide toddler rooms into four large areas: messy, dress-up, quiet, and large motor. Organize your messy activity space(s) near a water source on tiled flooring that can be easily cleaned.

Plan for quiet activities (such as looking at books or working on puzzles) to take place in a carpeted area so toddlers especially can work comfortably on the floor.

Locate the motor area on carpet and supplement 'fall zones' with padding so children won't get hurt during active play. As toddlers mature, you'll want to gradually introduce new areas and materials into your classroom, so make allowances for space when planning.

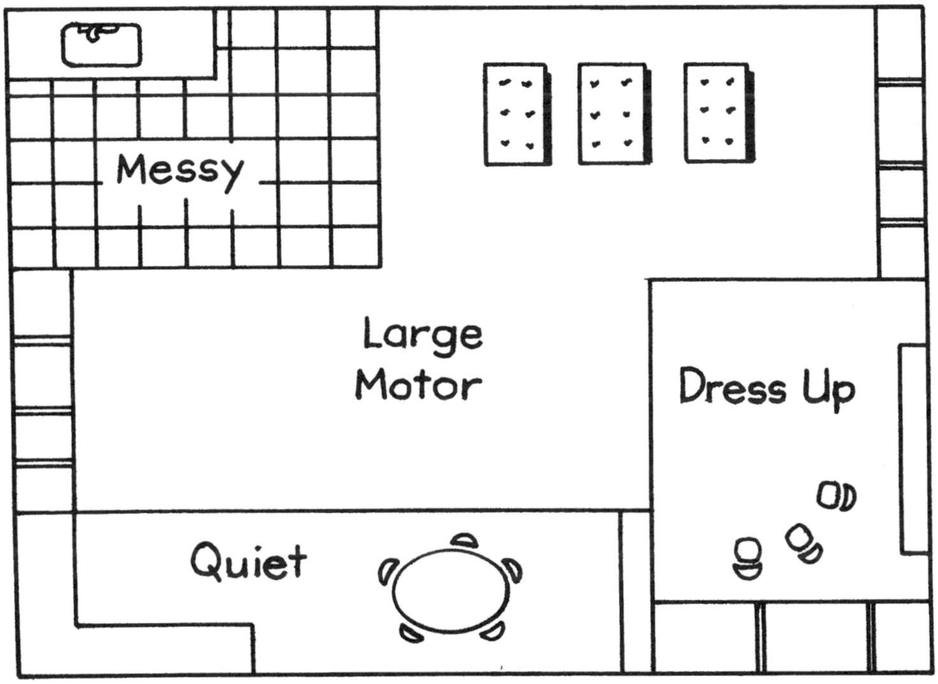

Preschool Rooms Begin by placing the Block Center in a carpeted corner. There should be only one "entrance" into this space, so structures won't be inadvertently knocked over.

Locate the Dramatic Play center next to the Block Center so interaction can occur between the two areas. These two centers take up almost half the room. Place other "active" areas (such as the Music Center and Woodworking Center) nearby. Plan to conduct group activities in the Block Center. If your Block Center is too small for group activities, it's probably too small overall.

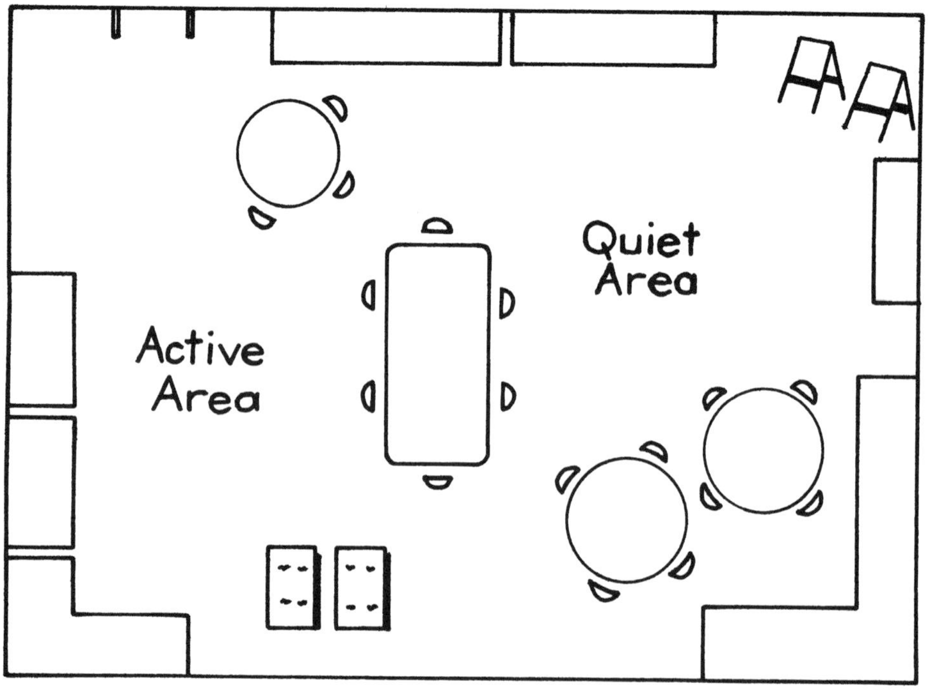

Store blocks and drama materials in built-in cabinets. Use dramatic play furniture, block shelves, screens, and pegboard dividers to separate areas.

Group together quieter areas, such as Language Arts, Creative Art, Sensory, and Discovery centers. The area by the door is a good place to greet children and parents in the morning and to prepare them to go home after school is over. You can gather small groups here for a story or talk time. If there are two teachers in your classroom, divide the class in half for most group times. One half of the class can meet in the Block Area, the other half in the Language Arts Area.

Place the Table Games or Manipulatives Center in the middle of the room. It acts as a buffer between the quieter areas and the more active areas. This arrangement also precludes a large empty area in the middle of the room for large motor movement.

3. Select Appropriate Materials

After you have thoroughly examined your room and made some general design plans, consider what specific interest or learning centers you will use. The selection of interest centers will indirectly determine what activities children will engage in throughout the year.

Interest centers might include the following:

- Creative Art
- Blocks
- Discovery
- Dramatic Play
- Language Arts (writing, reading, listening)
- Music and Movement
- Table Games
- Sensory
- Woodworking
- Surprise (This center will change focus according to the current interests of the children.)
- Spaces to display children's completed work
- Space to store ongoing projects.

Base your planning on developmentally appropriate practices by first considering your age group. Plan for all domains of development: language, cognitive, physical, and social-emotional. As you observe children playing in the various centers, you'll see how materials can be better adapted to individual children. You will also develop insights about children's interests and experiences to use for further planning.

Chapter Checklist

	Yes	No
1. Have I considered the age of my children when planning the room arrangement?		
2. Have I grouped noisy centers together?		
3. Have I grouped quiet centers together?		
4. Have I located certain centers near each other to encourage interaction?		
5. Have I provided storage space for items that are not being used?		
6. Have I provided appropriate space for individual centers?		
7. When choosing equipment, furnishings, and materials, have I considered the ages and developmental levels of my children?		
8. Have I provided space for displaying materials to encourage self-direction?		
9. Have I provided places and spaces to display finished products, to save items, or to set aside things to work on later?		

Chapter 5 offers guidelines for the physical arrangement of each center.

2

Rebus Charts in Interest Centers

Interest centers organized around rebus charts encourage children to think and work for themselves and in cooperation with others. As children become more independent, you'll have more time to interact with them on an individual basis. In this chapter, you'll find detailed descriptions of how to set up interest centers, plus some sample rebus charts to copy and use for each center. Chapter 4 provides more information about making, displaying, and storing rebus charts.

Creating a Child-Centered Curriculum

The term *child-centered* refers to curriculum planned around children's experiences, interests, and learning styles. It's different from the traditional approach in which the teacher chooses topics and plans activities with minimal feedback from children. According to research, child-centered learning is extremely effective for this age group.

Here are some suggestions for making your program more child-centered.

1 Brainstorm a Broad Theme

Pinpoint some general topics you think children would enjoy; keeping the subject as broad as possible will encourage maximum input from your students.

2. Get Feedback from Children

Present one of the topics you've brainstormed to children, eliciting their thoughts and ideas and finding out what they already know about the subject. Make a chart with two columns labeled *What we want to know* and *What we know.*

3. Narrow Down Ideas

Review the list of ideas. Ask children more questions to further define areas of interest.

4. Apply Observations

Interview children individually to find out more about what they want to learn. Ask parents and other family members for their input. Think of the activities you notice children enjoying daily; consider integrating these activities into your units of study.

The Developmentally Appropriate Environment

Take into account the age of your children when planning curriculum. Young toddlers, older toddlers, and preschool children in different stages of development will require different approaches to material.

A room for young toddlers has four large areas: a messy area, a dress-up area, a quiet area, and a large motor area. Each area takes up approximately one-fourth of the room. As children mature, you'll want to gradually change and add learning centers to reflect children's growth. In other words, a room for older toddlers would have some (but not all) of the characteristics of a room for young preschoolers.

A room for preschoolers may have 6 to 10 interest centers that are easily recognized and well delineated. Special learning areas could include the following.

- Block Center
- Dramatic Play Center
- Creative Art Center
- Language Arts Center
- Discovery Center
- Sensory Center
- Table Games Center (sometimes called the Manipulative Center)
- Surprise Center

Planning Inclusive Curriculum

Check to make sure the activities you create are inclusive, reflecting not only the cultural backgrounds of all the children in your room, but those in society as a whole. Materials and activities within an anti-bias curriculum reflect a variety of racial and ethnic backgrounds. Children play with multicultural dolls in the Dramatic Play Area and paint with colors representing different skin tones in the Creative Arts area. Music from different cultures plays quietly in the background during some parts of the day. Parents visit the class on occasion to share favorite family recipes and traditions.

Toddler Interest Centers

For this age group, there are four play areas.

1 Large Motor Area

Set up this active, noisy area far from spaces where quiet activities take place. Try to find a spot that's carpeted and open, so children can move about with little risk of injury. Materials in this center might include soft blocks, large cardboard blocks, and accessories.

Children this age are just beginning to appreciate block building. At first, they'll merely carry the blocks around with them. Then they'll begin to stack blocks into towers. You may see some children at this age make enclosures, but complex block-building doesn't usually happen until the preschool years.

Include low climbing and sliding structures, as well as push-pull toys, in this area. Be sure to incorporate an adequate 'fall zone' with protective padding around low climbing and sliding structures.

2. Dress-Up Area

Place housekeeping furniture in this area. Props might include anatomically correct dolls that represent a variety of ethnic backgrounds and races, as well as baby bottles, doll beds, plastic dishes, pots and pans, and empty food containers. Provide dress-up clothes like hats, shoes, purses, and vests. You may want to change the Dress-Up corner periodically to resemble one specific room. For example, one week that area could resemble a bedroom with pajamas, slippers, pillows, and books to read to dolls.

As you become aware of what's going on in children's lives, add the appropriate props to the Dress-Up area to help them further explore and reflect on experiences. For example, after a child has been to the hospital, place some simple "doctor" toys and clothes in this area.

3. Messy Area

Designate this as the area in which children can explore water, creative arts, and sensory activities. Locate messy activities near a faucet, sink, or other water source. Also, try organizing the area around a tile floor for easy cleanups.

Creative art materials in the Messy area could include different types of paper, "fat" crayons, large water-based markers, play dough, an easel with large brushes, paste, scraps of materials, and preschool scissors. All materials should be non-toxic.

Tape a large piece of butcher paper or newspaper onto the art table to make cleanup as easy as possible. Tie crayons, scissors, and other materials to the legs of the table so they're exactly where children can find them each time.

This is a good spot to display "discovery" materials like rocks, pieces of bark, shells, color paddles, various noisemakers, and sensory boxes that enable children to sample interesting textures (cotton, sand, natural sponges, coral).

Be sure smocks are available for all messy materials.

4. Quiet Area

This area should be padded with carpeting, soft pillows, and quilts or comforters. Activities include looking at books, doing puzzles, and playing with manipulatives. Daydreaming should also be encouraged!

Preschool Interest Centers

There are 8 basic centers for preschool children.

1 Block Center

Block play is one of the most beneficial play activities in an early childhood classroom. The Block Center is an active, noisy place, so locate it near other active areas, preferably in a carpeted corner in a low-traffic area. Placing the Block Center adjacent to the Dramatic Play Center allows children in these areas to interact with each other and combine activities. The Block Center and the Dramatic Play Center should take up at least one-third of your room.

Appropriate materials for this center would include large, hollow wooden blocks as well as one full set of wooden unit blocks. Make sure that there are plenty of blocks to play with so children don't become too impatient waiting for a turn.

Try introducing one type of block at a time to this center to give children an opportunity to feel mastery at manipulating new materials. This also allows you to observe how children deal with novelty through the following mediums:

- **Exploratory play**. Children physically explore and experiment with the blocks, moving them, looking at them, and touching them.
- **Practice play**. Children continue experimenting with the blocks, but with more stacking and building.
- **Symbolic play**. Children use the blocks to build houses, barns, office buildings, or castles.

Other appropriate materials for the block corner include hats, fishing poles, wooden and plastic figures (people and animals), and dollhouse furniture.

Small manipulative materials, such as Legos™ and Marbleworks™, should be placed in the Manipulative Center to avoid conflicts between children who want to play with these manipulatives and children who want floor space to build with blocks.

To promote independence in block areas, follow these suggestions.

Mark off the specific area with a rebus or mobile.

Use the open/closed sign and simple symbol charts for activities.

Use cues or shelf indicators to show children where blocks and block accessories belong. Start with cues that are the same size and shape as the blocks and boxes. When the children understand these cues, use smaller cues to suggest relative sizes and shapes.

For older children, use different-sized dots or other shapes to indicate various sizes of hollow blocks or accessories. For example, the largest hollow block may be represented by a large dot, the middle-sized blocks by a smaller dot, and the smallest blocks by the smallest dot.

Display pictures to remind children of activities they've done or topics you're studying that could be carried over into block building. For example, children might want to build train stations if you're studying transportation.

Store blocks on open shelves instead of in boxes to encourage self-direction in cleanup.

If possible, allow for two block areas. Locate one of the areas near the Dramatic Place Center and the other on the far side of the block storage area.

Provide a sign-up sheet where children can indicate that they are waiting their turn to play in the Block Center.

Set up related activities in the Block Center and Dramatic Play Center some of the time. For example, arrange an actor's dressing room in the Dramatic Play Center and a theater in the Block Center.

Encourage girls and boys to play in the Block Center by hanging photographs or posters that show both genders engaged in building activities.

2. Dramatic Play Center

At the beginning of the year provide housekeeping materials in the Dramatic Play Center. For toddlers, housekeeping materials could remain the focus throughout the year. As you notice individual preferences or when the class is motivated by a unit of study, add appropriate props.

Preschool children have wider experiences than toddlers, and the Dramatic Play Center should reflect those experiences. Note children's interests to determine how and when to change the dramatic play setup and props. Use the things children discuss in sharing circles to determine the theme of your Dramatic Play area. If children continue to be interested in construction, set up Dramatic Play as a construction site. Some other possibilities are a restaurant, flower shop, farmhouse/barn, or picnic in the woods.

The following are suggestions for indirect guidance in the Dramatic Play Center.

Make a mobile or Dramatic Play Center marker to correspond with the topic of exploration.

Display pictures and symbols to indicate the types of activities children could try.

Coordinate activities with the Block Center to encourage complementary use of both areas.

Stimulate imagination by making a variety of materials and costumes available. For example, suggest a laundromat by placing a basket of clothes and some pictures of clothes or laundry in the area, but let children decide to make the toy kitchen sink into a "washing machine" and the toy stove into a "dryer."

Outline dishes and utensils on shelf paper so the items can be returned to their proper places.

Outline clothing on a pegboard to suggest where to hang dress-up clothes or the clothes for "sale" in the clothing store. Outlines or pictures of pots and pans would suggest where these might hang in the kitchen or in a restaurant.

Use pictures or unusual boxes to store materials for individual situations. For example, store restaurant materials in a gallon ice cream carton covered with a placemat or menu. Use an airline's timetable to cover a box of travel items.

Cue prop boxes according to the items they contain. A box containing hats might be cued with a sketch of several hats. A box of vests might be cued with magazine pictures of community helpers such as an office worker, doctor, pilot, bus driver, or teacher. Designate a box of aprons with pictures of a baker, gardener, cook, waiter, florist, or a carpenter. You can easily make some of these versatile vests and aprons from a small piece of doubled fabric (16" to 18").

Follow these steps to make the vests:

1. Cut off slack legs at the knee (approximately 13" from knee to cuff). Open both side seams on one leg, and one seam on the other leg. Retain the hem of the slacks for the hem of the vest.

2. Lay large piece on bottom and other two on top with the right sides of the fabric facing. Match side seams.

3. Cut out a neckline and armholes as shown in the illustration on the next page. Sew side and shoulder seams.

4. Turn under and sew the cut edge to make a facing for fasteners.

5. Add buttons and buttonholes, snaps, gripper snaps, a zipper, Velcro®, or ties.

6. Add pockets and trim as desired.

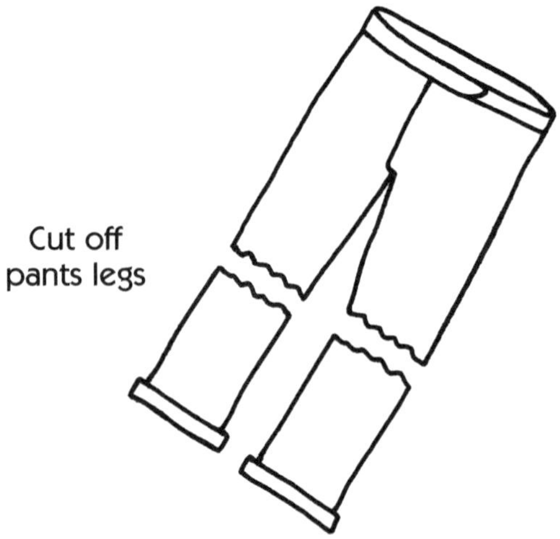

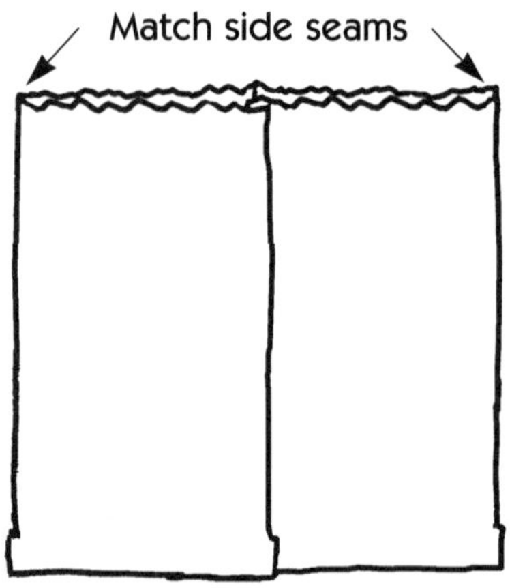

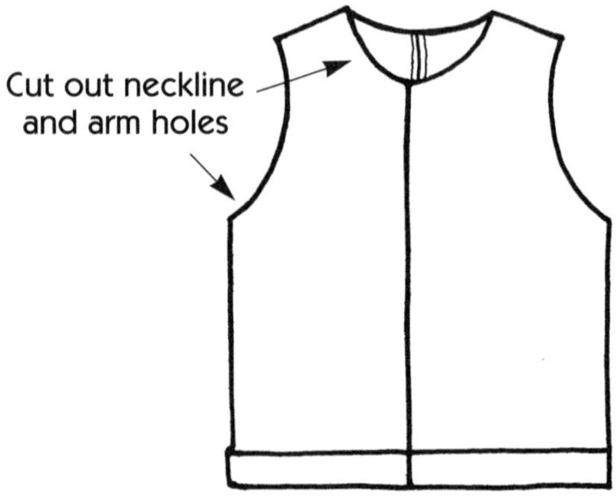

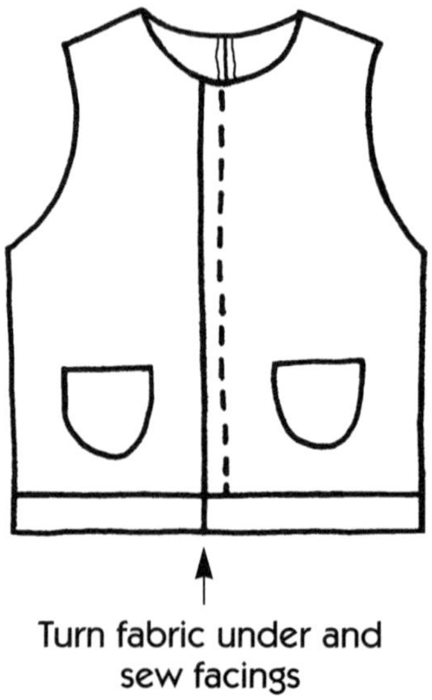

Child-sized aprons are useful for dress-up clothes, art aprons, or cooking aprons. Two aprons can be made from one pair of slacks.

Follow these steps to make your own aprons:

1. Cut off slack legs at the knees (approximately 17" from knee to cuff).

2. Open one seam. Fold fabric at other seam, and cut armholes as shown in the illustration, retaining the bottom hem for the hem of the apron.

3. Fold under at top for facing. Add a piece of elastic at the neck line so it will stretch over the children's heads and adjust to a variety of sizes.

4. Add a wraparound tie that will close in the front with a tie, a button, gripper snap, snap, or Velcro. You can make a tie from the leftover material from the pants or use other scrap material you may have on hand.

5. Use fabric from the upper part of the pants for pockets; add trim to correspond with an occupation, if desired.

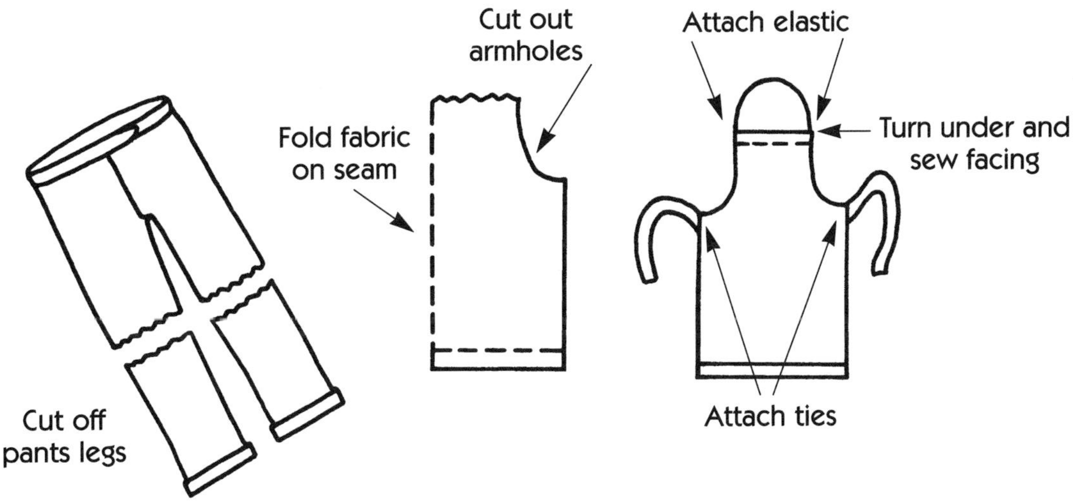

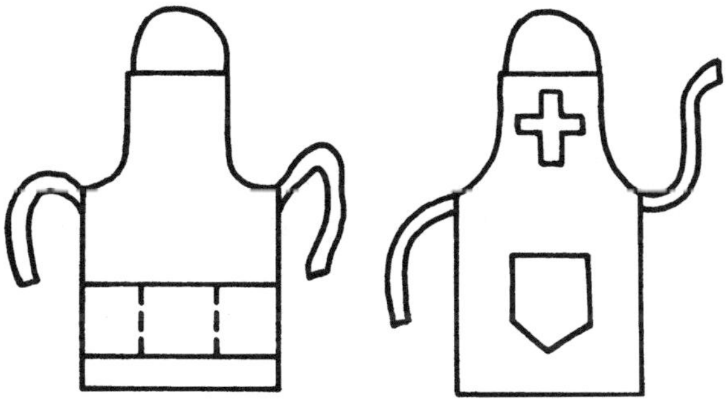

Variations

This chapter includes a rebus called *Putting Clothes Away*. Make rebus charts for other household activities, such as:

- washing or scraping dishes
- vacuuming and dusting
- bathing a doll

Bring in a large box and a barrel. Observe how the children use them in dramatic play. When children offer a constructive suggestion for using these items, develop a dramatic play activity to go along with it.

3. Creative Art Center

The Creative Art Center should be near a source of water with flooring that can be easily cleaned. Tables are necessary for finger painting, collage, clay, and other projects. Provide a shelf area for storage and display areas for art projects. Be sure to display art throughout the room, not just in the creative art area. These display areas can include the room, the hall, and even the ceiling. Some classrooms have a specific area for each child to display art.

Set up easels with fresh paper or works-in-progress. You can make an easel from three sections of a large cardboard box. The display easel described in Chapter 4 can be adapted to make a table easel. Place a box next to or under the easel to hold paper. Be sure that children can manipulate these materials without having to ask for adult help.

Take art activities outside daily. A fence or a wall makes an ideal painting surface. Try finding a spot for a permanent outdoor easel. (See Chapter 10, Using Outdoor Interest Centers.)

When choosing materials to place on the art shelves, think about colors, textures, and materials that children can use in many ways. Preschool children enjoy using a wide variety of materials in their art work: crayons, markers, scissors, construction paper, paste, glue, and collage materials. Avoid planning the final product. Let children think of how they'd like to start, but encourage them to change directions as their ideas evolve and they experiment with materials.

The following suggestions offer ideas for indirect guidance in the Creative Art center.

Make an art mobile or interest-center marker to indicate the Art Center.

Use simple symbols and rebus charts for activities and open/ closed signs to indicate if the Art Center is available for use.

Use cues or indicators on shelves to show children where items belong. Cue individual trays or boxes of materials for particular activities, such as finger painting.

Provide smocks that children can put on by themselves. Make them from old hand towels or flannel-backed material.

Here's how.

1. Cut a slit for the neck.
2. Add a small vertical slit to the neck opening so the smock will go over the child's head.
3. Bind the opening.
4. Add short ties at the sides of the back that will fasten in front with a button, snap, or velcro, or add a longer tie for tying around the child's waist.

Provide rebus charts for art projects. At the end of this chapter, you'll find sample charts for the following art activities and mediums:

- Play Dough
- Finger Painting
- Mixing Paint
- Easel Painting
- Cleaning Paint Brushes
- Blob Painting
- Object Printing
- Collage

Place rebus charts in a convenient location so that children will be responsible for cleaning brushes, mixing paint, and washing tables. (See charts at end of chapter.)

Arrange display devices for art rebus charts (Chapter 4).

Provide self-help art supplies such as:

- A box for paper near or under the easels;
- Trays or tubs of cued art supplies easily managed by children;
- Clothespins or strips of tape for holding paper on easels, or prepunched paper to fit over nails on easels;
- A drying rack on which paintings can be draped to dry, or a newspaper-lined drying space on the floor.

Try some of the art activities using the rebus charts provided in this chapter.

4. Discovery Center

Math/Science/Nature Activities

In this area, children uses their senses and thinking skills to test and investigate ideas and figure out new ways to use materials.

Use your Discovery Area as a place to display new materials that children will be using in other centers or as part of other activities. For example, if you plan on setting up the Dramatic Play Area as a doctor's office, you can introduce items such as a stethoscope in the Discovery Area. Give children time to approach the new items and experiment with them before showing exactly how they're used. Next, let children practice what you've taught them about the objects. Finally, show children that you are going to place objects in specific centers so they can experiment even more.

There may also be some permanent items in this area, such as a class pet, some plants, and a few shells. Also encourage children to bring items from home to display.

If you do not have a separate Sensory Area, place sensory materials in this area. A commercial water and sand table is good, but the kind of small plastic tub used for washing dishes works well, too. Birdseed, shaving cream, hard pasta noodles, dried cat or dog food, and, of course, sand and water are also good sensory materials.

At the end of this chapter, you'll find rebus charts for this center.

The following suggestions offer ideas for indirect guidance in the Discovery Center.

Make a mobile or marker for the area.

Display pictures and symbols relating to nature, science, measuring, weighing, and comparing.

Display a large question mark to show that asking questions is an important part of making discoveries. Add an eye and a hand symbol to suggest that children *look, touch,* and *do.*

Include many testing or investigative activities where children have to predict what will happen when they try an activity, as well as ways to check their predictions. Make rebus charts explaining the experiments. This chapter includes rebus charts for Bubble Blowing, Absorption, Color Mixing, Float or Sink, Will It Attract, and Water Mixing.

Use the "open/closed" and "yes/no" symbols in the center.

Provide cued box lids or trays to hold materials.

Include some egg cartons, ice cube trays, or other divided containers for classification activities.

Provide a low table with comfortable chairs.

Place magnets, magnifying glasses, prisms, scales, rulers, and other science- and math-related items on a cued shelf in the Discovery Center. Decorate a storage box with a space or other science-related theme.

If you have a class pet, display a story children have dictated, as well as the animal's name, on the cage.

5. COOKING CENTER

Cooking activities can take place in the Discovery Center, but if you're lucky enough to have a large room, you can have a separate Cooking Center.

Cooking may be an interest center activity or a group experience. Young children benefit more from a cooking experience if the group is small and if each child has a chance to participate. However, there are some cooking experiences that lend themselves to prior demonstration. In this case, you might show children the process, but give them the opportunity to follow the rebus and do the activity on their own.

Safety is important in cooking. Any time a hot item, an electrical appliance, or sharp utensils are used, be sure an adult is supervising. Use the rebus charts at the end of this chapter to get started.

Cooking with Older Toddlers Begin with very simple cooking activities, such as Ants on a Log (peanut butter on celery, sprinkled with raisins). Toddlers can easily tear up lettuce for salad, but cut and grate carrots and other vegetables ahead of time.

Cooking with Preschoolers Preschoolers will enjoy simple cooking activities, but as they mature, they can handle more complex cooking utensils. Electric skillets and blenders can be used if there's constant adult supervision.

The following are ideas for self-direction and indirect guidance in the Cooking Center.

Make a marker or mobile to display on the days when you're doing a cooking project.

When cooking is planned, display the hand-washing and smock rebuses. Remind children to follow the instructions on the rebus.

Begin with simple cooking projects and advance to more complicated ones. Children in a full-day program will enjoy making items from the school lunch menu. Children in a half-day program can make snack items and occasional special meals.

Plan the activities so that all children get an opportunity to participate. Different groups of children can participate at various times.

Outline each cooking utensil on a chart or pegboard and hang where children can reach them.

Draw outlines of utensils and cooking supplies on tray liners so that they can be neatly returned.

Mark cups and bowls to indicate quantities.

Use graduated cups for measuring dry ingredients.

Prepare food so children can perform tasks easily. For example, cut a flat side away from an apple to keep it steady before helping children cut their own slices.

Pre-measure ingredients for beginning cooks. Later the children can measure from a full container.

Emphasize nutrition when planning cooking activities. Young children learn to eat a variety of foods if they are exposed to them without prejudice.

Teach children to use sugar and salt in moderation. Include fresh vegetables and fruits as regular snack items.

Gather all necessary materials before beginning a recipe.

Begin with simple cooking rebus charts. Enlarge rebus drawings to show one step per 8 1/2" x 11" page. Advance to more complex rebus charts as the children become more experienced. Show more charts per page, with the drawings ordered in sequence.

Use *realistic* drawings of ingredients, processes, and utensils that indicate items to be used in the recipe. Color the drawings to match the real items. See charts at the end of this chapter.

Make an illustrated menu to go with the recipes so children make associations between words and names of foods.

6. LANGUAGE ARTS CENTER

Reading/Writing/Listening

Locate the Language Arts Center in the quietest part of the room. Divide the area into three distinct but related activity areas. The Reading Area could include books, shelves, and a soft place to sit. This area can be relatively small, since only two or three children and one adult would be in this area at one time.

In the Writing Area, provide a small table, two chairs, and materials such as paper, pencils, a hole punch, scissors, tape, and stapler.

In the Listening Area, supply a tape player with a headset, a selection of taped stories, and companion books so that children can follow along. You don't need to buy tapes; try making your own or ask special guest hosts (like your center director) to tape a book for children.

Here are some ideas for self-direction and indirect guidance in the Language Arts Center.

Make a mobile or marker.

Use symbols to indicate *look, listen,* or *do.*

Provide a rocking chair, some pillows, and a cozy hideaway to encourage quiet activities. The hideaway could be a cardboard refrigerator box with doors and windows cut into it, an easel with a lightweight blanket over it, or a card table draped with a sheet.

Cue the tape recorder by placing a green piece of tape on the *start* switch and a red piece on the *stop* switch. Use arrows to point out the direction of the volume control.

Encourage storytelling and language development with puppets and a puppet theater or a flannel board with felt figures. You can make a theater from a box, table, or bookcase.

Use magazines and catalogs to make a picture file children can use for sorting and storytelling activities. Mount pictures on cardboard, laminate or cover them with adhesive-backed vinyl, and store in a box with dividers. Children will learn filing and classification skills as they get a picture from the file, talk about it, put it up for display, and then return it to its proper location.

Add shelf markers to indicate where materials belong.

Make a guessing box to stimulate language. Cut a hole in the top of a shoe box and place objects inside. Children put their hands in the hole and try to guess what the objects are. Change objects frequently.

Make a rebus chart or sign that suggests how children should handle books and put them away.

Place new materials in the Language Arts Center as various topics are introduced.

7. TABLE GAMES CENTER

Include puzzles, shape boxes, visual-motor toys, games, and manipulatives in this area. In addition to store-bought materials, provide teacher-made matching and board games.

The following are suggestions for indirect guidance in the Table Games Center.

Make a mobile or marker.

Use pictures and action symbols as directions for activities.

Don't put out too many items at once; children may have trouble choosing among many possibilities.

If the floor isn't carpeted, provide carpet squares on which children can play games.

Include a small table or two in your game center.

Make or purchase some trays for games so children can keep all the materials together. Box lids or baskets can also be used for this purpose.

Cue instructions to the games with rebuses whenever possible.

Ask questions that encourage children to use thinking skills to solve puzzles and play games. Ask *Why? How? What do you think might happen?* and *What else can you think of to do with that?*

Draw outlines around games and table toys on the shelves so children know where to return them.

Include games that involve matching, finding patterns, and classifying objects.

Include several guessing boxes. Children find the object and use it in a specific way by playing with it, discussing it, or matching it one-to-one with a symbol or other representation. For example, children could be challenged to match one lid to another or to a symbol that represents all metal things. Children can check correct responses on the other side of rebus cards.

8. Rotating Centers

Use special interest centers from time to time to reinforce specific themes you're studying or concepts children are beginning to master. If you have a large classroom, you might plan a space for a weekly "surprise center." Variety keeps children interested.

Outdoor Interest Centers

Consider your outdoor play area as an extension of the classroom. The outdoors can be one of your greatest learning laboratories!

Children participate in activities differently outdoors than inside. With fewer restraints, children feel freer to move around, make noise, and role play. A child who seems easily distracted indoors may blossom into a real leader on the playground.

Even in rainy weather, children can learn about weather, trees, leaves, gardens, and animals. A walk in the rain (with proper protective clothing) is an excellent way to discover the wonders of nature. Involve children in deciding what materials and equipment are safe to use after a rainstorm when the playground is still wet.

Refer to Chapter 2 for rebuses to accompany many of the activities that you plan for outdoor time.

YOUR ROLE Teachers can be great models for how to enjoy the outdoors. Watch how children respond when you maneuver an obstacle course, play musical instruments, or examine interesting rocks. Your willingness to explore will encourage a timid child to climb a little higher or to try a new piece of equipment.

Children of all ages benefit from outdoor play. Take young infants outside in carts or strollers; place them on blankets under a shady tree and let them feel the breeze on their skin and look at leaves as they move against the blue sky. As their visual skills improve, point out the movement of the clouds. A playground for mobile infants should be challenging but safe. Encourage infants to experience the feel of grass and sand (watching carefully so they don't "eat" unsafe materials). Brightly colored toys and even a rocker can provide extra stimulation and comfort outside.

The following are 6 suggestions for outdoor interest centers.

1. OUTDOOR DISCOVERY ZONES*

Take a tour of the playground and divide it into zones appropriate for different age groups and types of projects. When planning for toddlers, remember that children this age are unable to share; provide duplicates of favorite items to avoid conflicts.

2. Dramatic Play Zone

Use playhouses, wheeled vehicles, and assorted props to reinforce parallel, associative, and imaginative play.

Develop dramatic play prop boxes to leave in outdoor storage areas. Dramatic play boxes for preschoolers could include dress-up clothing and camping equipment (tent, sleeping bags, cook stove, campfire), garage props, or garden tools. Other ideas for outdoor themes you could develop include spaceships, transportation, an ice cream stand, and a circus or zoo.

Plain cardboard boxes are excellent for encouraging pretend play outdoors. Housekeeping furniture and cooking utensils in a sandbox are perfect for make-believe cooking.

Stripped down cars or boats, or a steering wheel mounted in a wooden box are valuable pieces of outdoor dramatic play equipment. Just make sure any metals have been sanded and are rust free.

3. Construction Zone

Provide a workbench with real tools and soft wood. There should also be a variety of construction materials that do not require tools: outdoor blocks, wooden planks, plastic and wooden boxes, small cable spools, old tires from different vehicles, barrels, sawhorses, and pulleys. Provide a cued pegboard for storage of tools.

*The information about outdoor zones is based on materials prepared by Sandy Enders in the Child Development Department at San Antonio College.

Sequence the introduction of construction materials to meet children's developmental needs. Young three-year-olds can pound golf tees into Styrofoam™ with a plastic or wooden hammer. Children with good eye-hand coordination will be ready to pound pre-set nails you have set ahead of time into soft wood.

A sturdy workbench with clamps can hold wood for sawing. Naturally, any time children are using clamps or saws, an adult must be nearby to supervise. Provide goggles to protect eyes (the number of goggles available will remind children how many people may play at the center at one time). Be sure to give children some lessons in using tools safely before introducing ANY of these materials.

4. Active Play Zone

The needs of toddlers and preschoolers are different in the Active Play Zones.

Toddlers To encourage independent activity, toddler play structures must be low to the ground and spread out for children who are practicing climbing and sliding skills. Provide push-pull toys and wide ramps and places to climb.

Preschoolers Children this age like to ride tricycles, climb structures, jump, crawl through tunnels, bounce, slide, and play with a parachute or big playground balls. A large open area is ideal for these activities.

An obstacle course is an excellent activity for self-directed learning. Obstacle courses teach many concepts like *under, around, behind, next to, in,* and *out*. Reinforce these ideas as you interact with children. Also introduce temporal words such as *first, next,* and *last*.

Cue these courses by using footprint and hand print symbols. Arrange some tires in a circular or snakelike pattern so children can step or jump into and out of them. Add a tunnel made from barrels, a walking beam or balance board, and a ball to bounce in and out of a tire or box.

Ask children to help set up obstacle courses, too. Draw a diagram of the course on a piece of poster board and put it up outside. Next time, see if children will arrange the course themselves. Encourage changes and draw a new diagram for each new course.

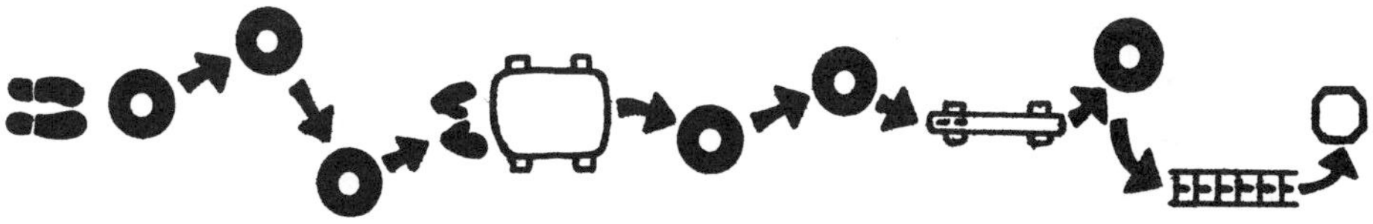

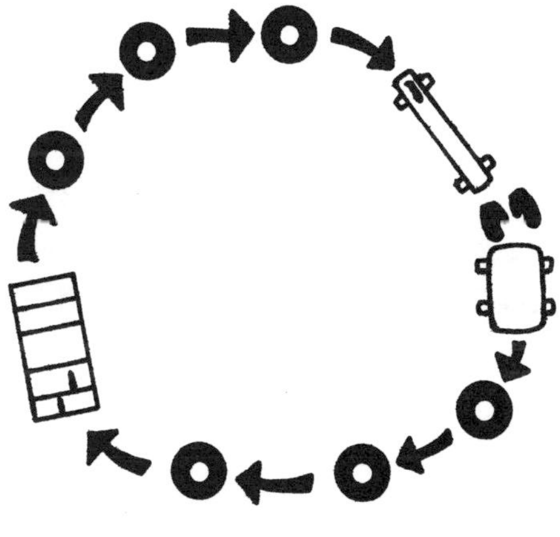

Set up a board or box as a Beanbag Toss (see rebus at the end of this chapter). Be sure children understand that it is their responsibility to return the beanbags to the proper container when they finish using them.

- **U**se the Beanbag Toss rebus chart, but ask the children what other materials could be used as well. Display their suggestions on the rebus chart.
- **A**dapt the board for children with less-developed motor skills by making only one hole. Alter the rebus chart accordingly.

- Tie this activity to a classroom theme by decorating it appropriately. For instance, to reflect a zoo or circus theme, paint a lion's mouth around one of the holes.

See the end of this chapter for a sample beanbag toss rebus.

If there's an outdoor electrical outlet available, use a heavy-duty extension cord to play songs on a record player or tape recorder. Or use battery-operated equipment. Even without electrical equipment, children can play musical games like "London Bridge," "La Vibora de la Mar," and "Here We Go Round the Mulberry Bush." And where better to try out different musical instruments than outside, where children can be as noisy as they want!

Finally, in hot weather, suggest that the children bring swimsuits to school. Young children enjoy a wading pool, running through spray from a garden hose, or playing in mud.

5. NATURE ZONE

The Nature Zone should be a setting where children can experience nature close up. Provide a sensory-rich environment for either toddlers or preschoolers by locating the zone among trees and plants, near water, large rocks, and boulders. Help children use real gardening tools to care for flowers, herbs, or vegetables in a special garden plot.

You can also house animals in this. Bird feeders and a birdbath will encourage a variety of local birds to come to the area.

6. Quiet Play Zone

In this zone, children can engage in quiet, restful activities or simply retreat from active play. It can contain tables and easels in a shady place located away from heavily trafficked areas. Here, toddlers and preschool children can participate in activities with paints, play dough, and fine-motor manipulatives. They can make nature collages and murals on fences or large cardboard boxes. Hang an old sheet from the fence and let children paint with tempera paint or water-based marking pens. Retrace designs with permanent markers to keep them fresh longer.

Provide discovery activities in this area (see chapter 2). In addition, provide magnifying glasses and binoculars to examine things near and far.

Bring library books, puppets, and table games outdoors. Rug squares or blankets provide an excellent place to read a story or play with puppets.

Water play is perfect for the outdoors. Bring several dish pans outside under a tree or other overhang and call attention to the activity by hanging a mobile and props (a bubble pipe, plastic bottle, and funnel) from a branch. Children can wear smocks made from old towels or, in warm weather, bathing suits.

For other sensory explorations, supply buckets or pans of sand, cornmeal, oatmeal, beans, or sawdust.

Finally, try ending outdoor play periods with quiet time. Children can gather to share ideas and evaluate the day before going in for lunch or leaving for the day.

CHAPTER CHECKLIST, PART 1

	Yes	No
1. Do I involve children in planning the curriculum?		
2. Do I change the materials in centers as the children's interests and skills change?		
3. Do the materials and the activities in my room reflect all ages, races, a variety of cultures, different kinds of families and children and adults with special needs?		
4. If I teach young toddlers, is my room divided into four large areas?		
5. If I teach older toddlers, does my room reflect the children's growth?		
6. If I teach preschool children, do I have at least six centers that children can easily recognize?		
7. Are shelves or other storage areas cued so children can easily return toys or items after play?		
8. Do some centers contain rebuses or pictures to help children use materials appropriately?		
9. Do I base some decisions about activities and materials on observations of children and information from parents?		
10. Do I expand the scope of my centers as the year goes on?		

CHAPTER CHECKLIST, PART 2

	Yes	No
1. Have I planned outdoor learning center activities as carefully as indoor activities?		
2. Have I planned ways to use the outdoor environment on rainy days?		
3. Do I interact with the children during outdoor time?		
4. If I work with infants, do I take them outdoors frequently and on a daily basis?		
5. If I work with toddlers or preschool children, have I provided a minimum of 45 minutes of outdoor time in the morning *and* in the afternoon?		
6. Do I provide a variety of developmentally appropriate activities in the Dramatic Play Zone?		
7. Do I provide a variety of developmentally appropriate activities in the Construction Zone?		
8. Do I provide a variety of developmentally appropriate activities in the Active Play Zone?		
9. Do I provide a variety of developmentally appropriate activities in the Nature Zone?		
10. Do I provide a variety of developmentally appropriate activities in the Quiet Zone?		

Putting Clothes Away

1

Hang up hats, coats, and dresses.

2

Fold shirts and put them in a drawer.

Make Play Dough

You will need:

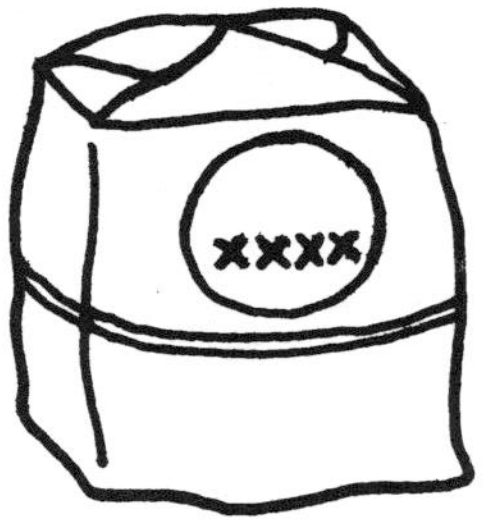
flour

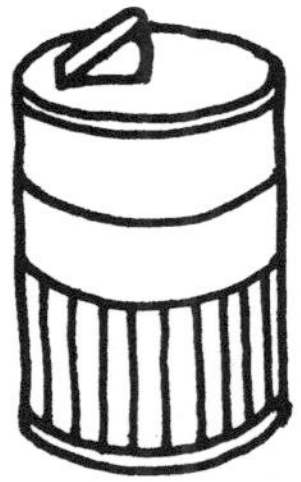
salt

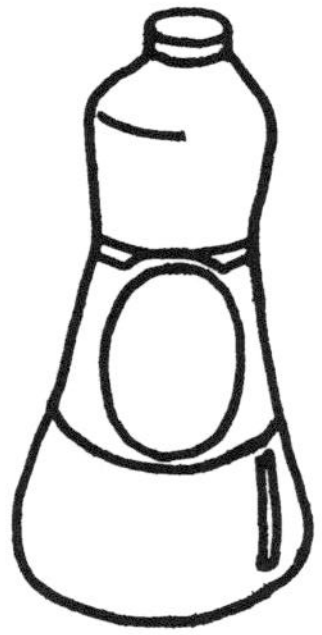
oil

cream of tartar

baking powder

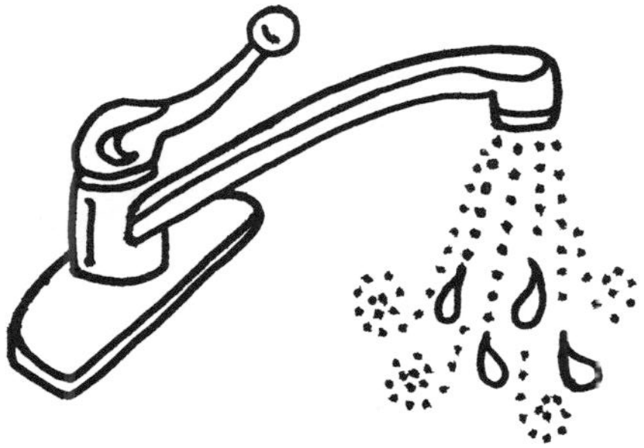
water

bowl

spoon

measuring cup

Make Play Dough

1

Put all ingredients
in a bowl.

2

Stir hard.

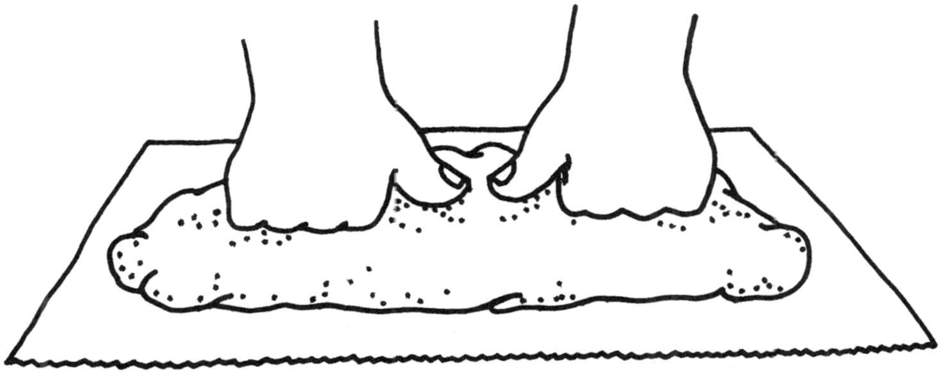

3

Turn out on waxed paper. Knead well.

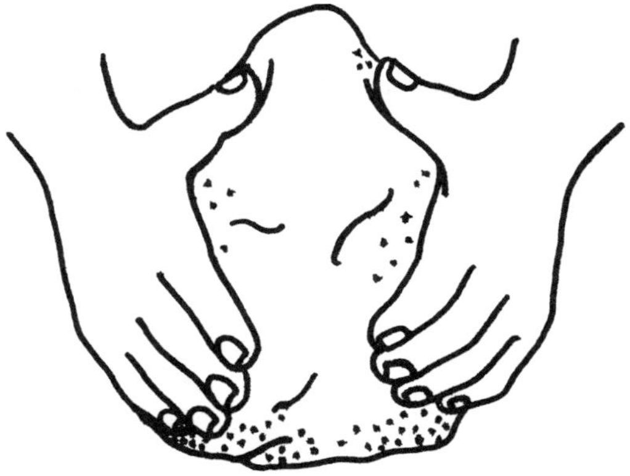

4

Play with the clay.

Finger Painting

1

Put paper on the table.

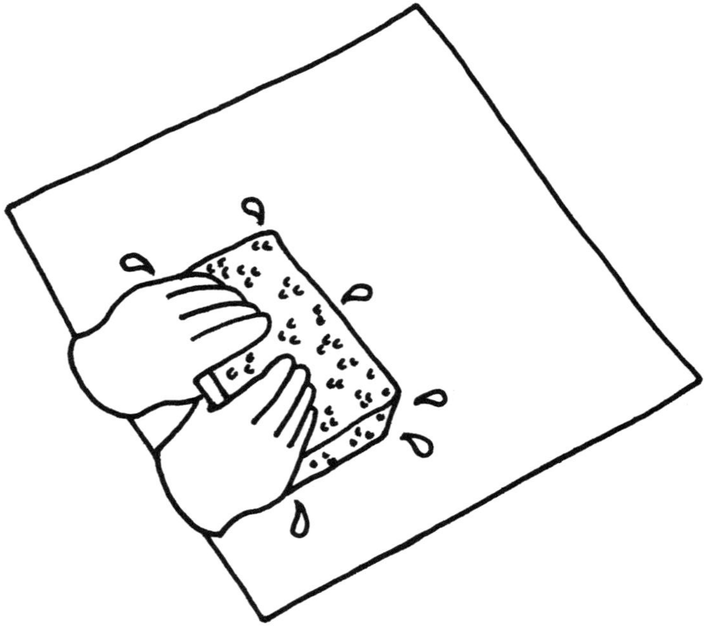

2

Wet the paper with a sponge.

Finger Painting

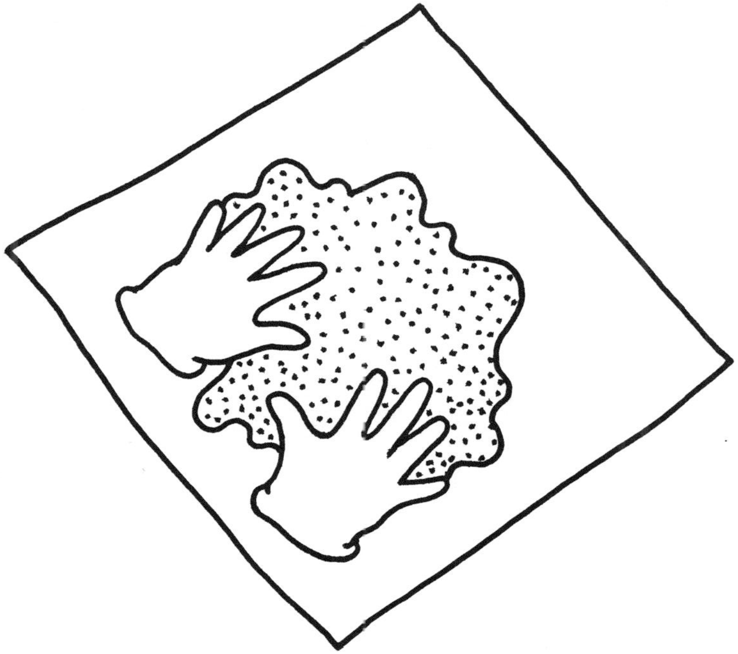

3

Paint picture.

4

Hang picture to dry.

Mixing Paint

1

Add 3 tablespoons paint.

2

Add water 1 teaspoon at a time.

Mixing Paint

3

Stir.

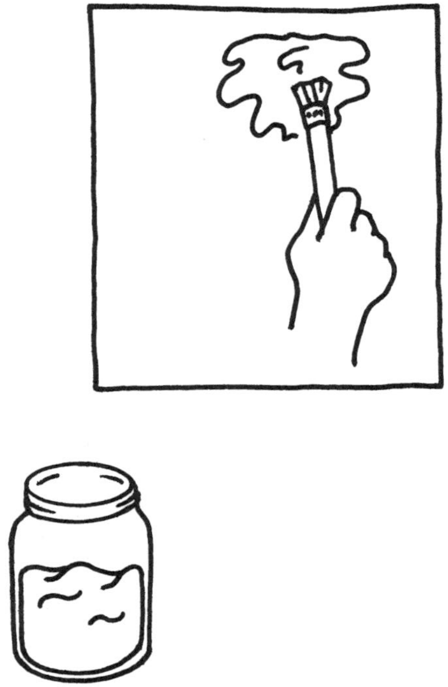

4

Paint.

Easel Painting

1

Put on a smock.

2

Put tape on paper.
Put paper on easel.

Easel Painting

3

Paint picture.

4

Hang picture to dry.

Easel Painting

5

Wash hands.

6

Hang smock on hook.

Cleaning Paint Brushes

1

Wash the paint brush.

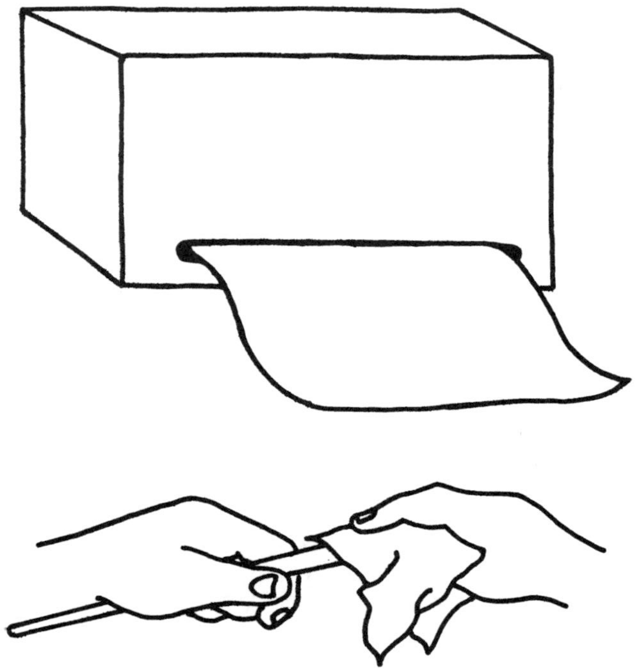

2

Dry the paint brush.

Cleaning Paint Brushes

3

Throw the towel in a trash can.

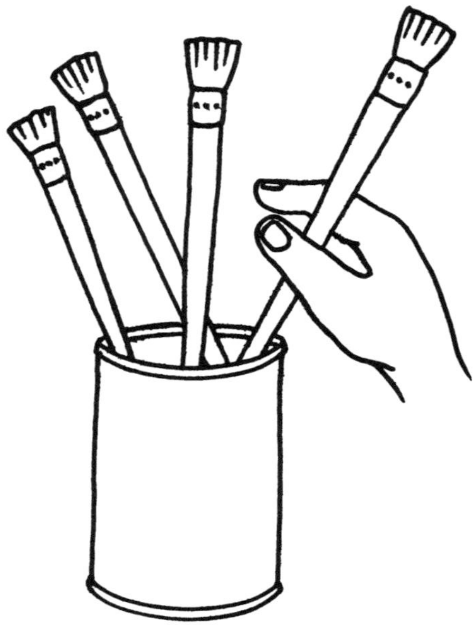

4

Stand the paint brush up in a can.

Blob Painting

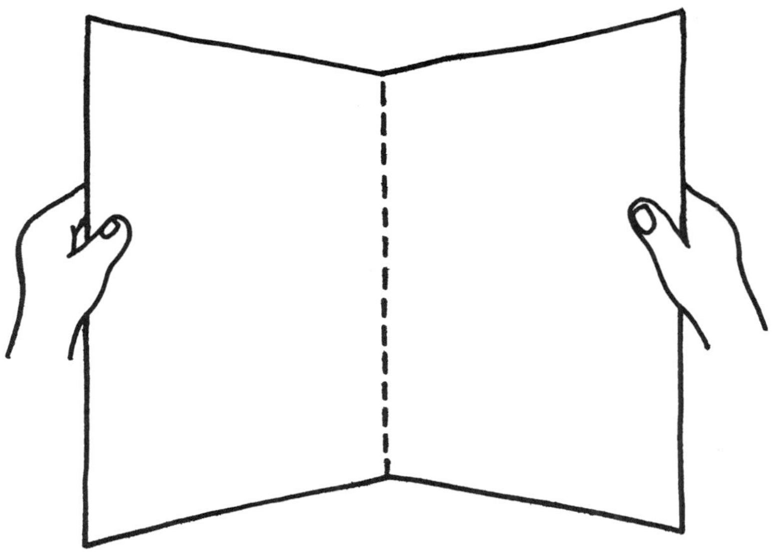

1

Fold the paper.

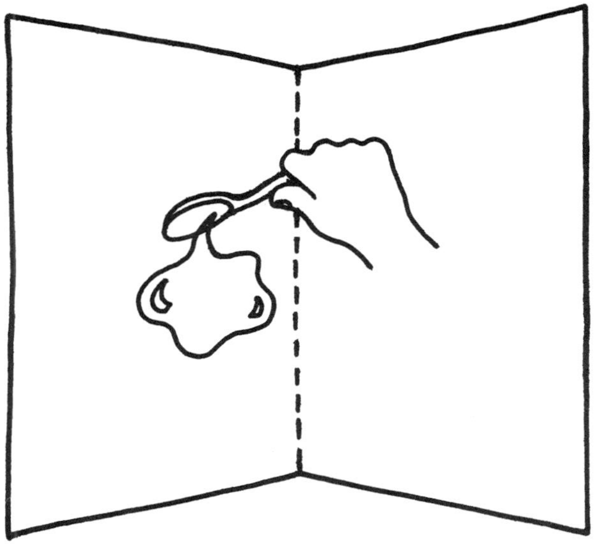

2

Spoon on the paint.

Blob Painting

3

Fold and press paper.

4

Open paper.

5

Hang picture to dry.

Object Printing

You will need:

coins
toy car
shape blocks

objects

paint

marker

paper

Object Printing

1

Dip objects
in paint.

2

Stamp objects
on paper.

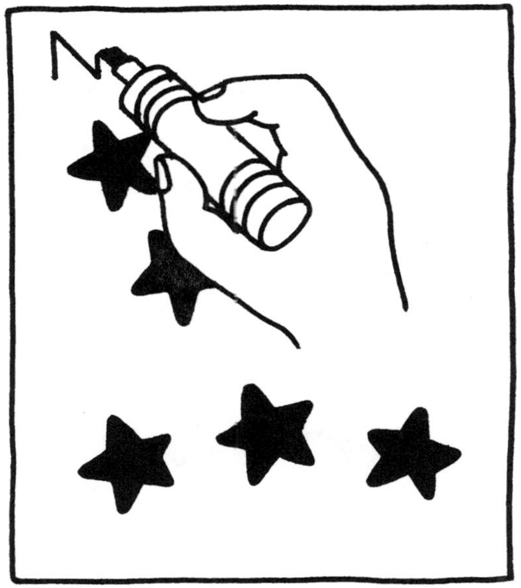

3

Write your name.

4

Hang your picture
to dry.

Collage

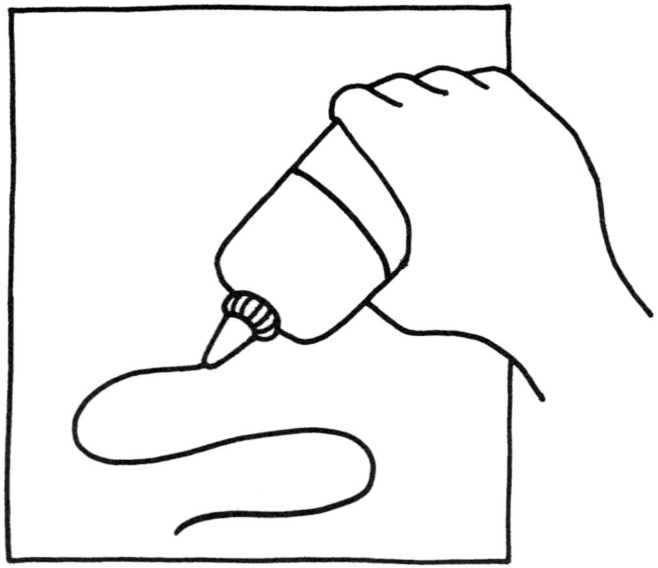

1

Put the glue on the paper.

2

Add bits of paper.

Collage

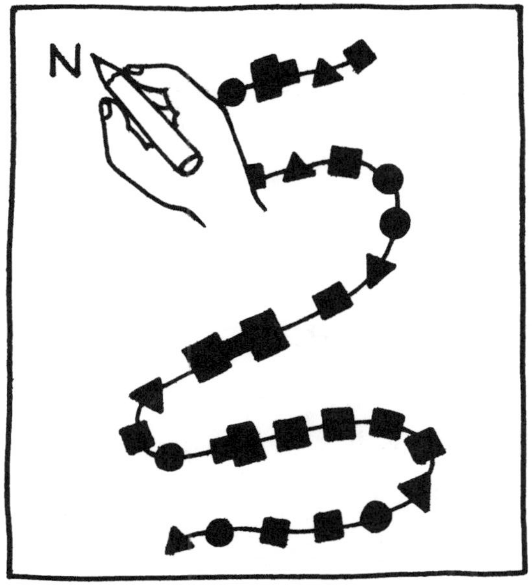

3

Write your name.

4

Hang your collage to dry.

Water-Mixing Experiment

You will need:

Water-Mixing Experiment

1

Add one spoonful of sand to one glass of water.

2

Stir with a spoon.

3

What happens to the sand in the water?

Water-Mixing Experiment

4

Add one spoonful of oil to one glass of water.

5

Stir with a spoon.

6

What happens to the oil in the water?

Bubble-Blowing Experiment

You will need:

water

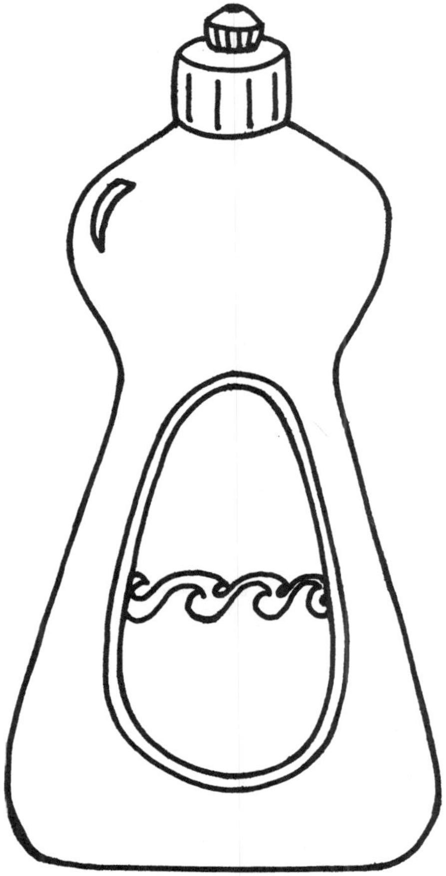

soap

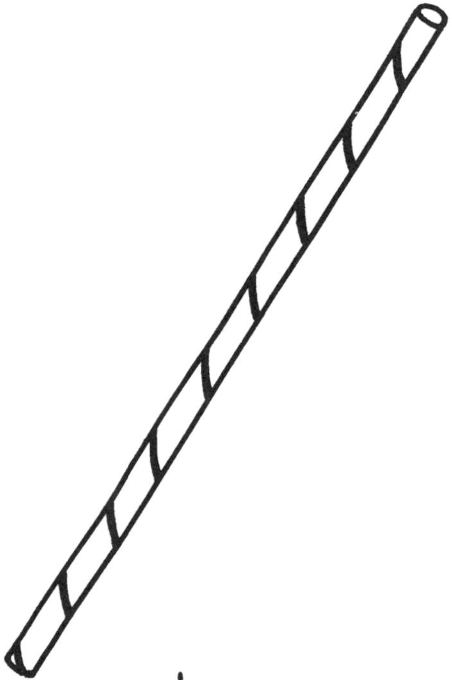

straw

Bubble-Blowing Experiment

1
Add soap to water.

2
Mix soap with water.

3
Blow in straw to make bubbles.

Absorption Experiment

You will need:

Absorption Experiment

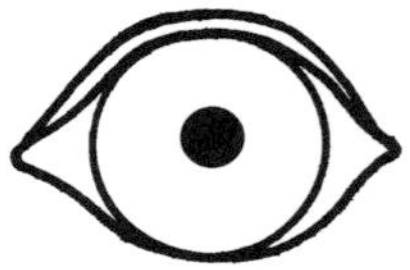

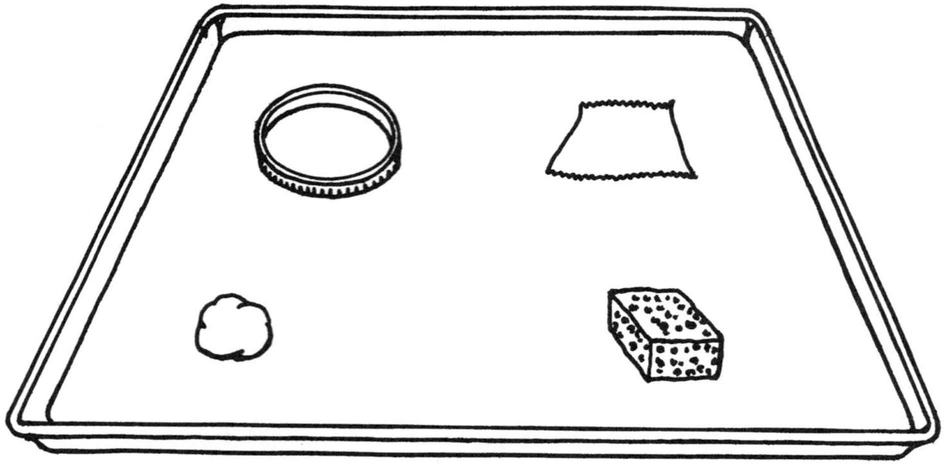

1

Look at these items. Which ones absorb, or take in, water?

2

Put them on the YES tray or the NO tray.

Absorption Experiment

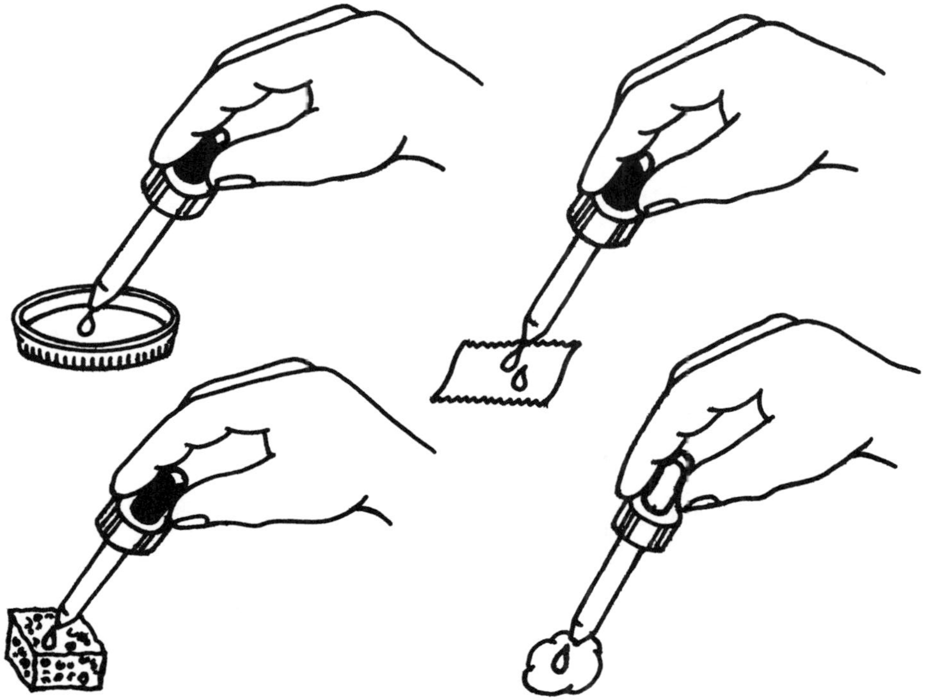

3

Drop water
from a dropper.

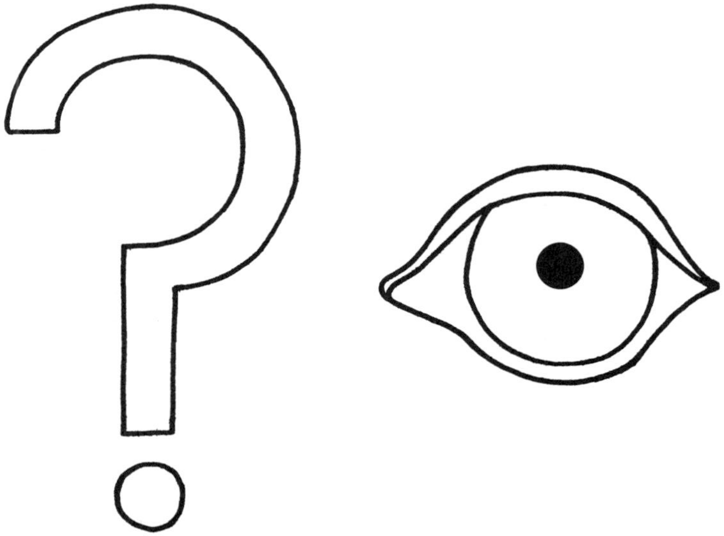

4

What happens?

Absorption Experiment

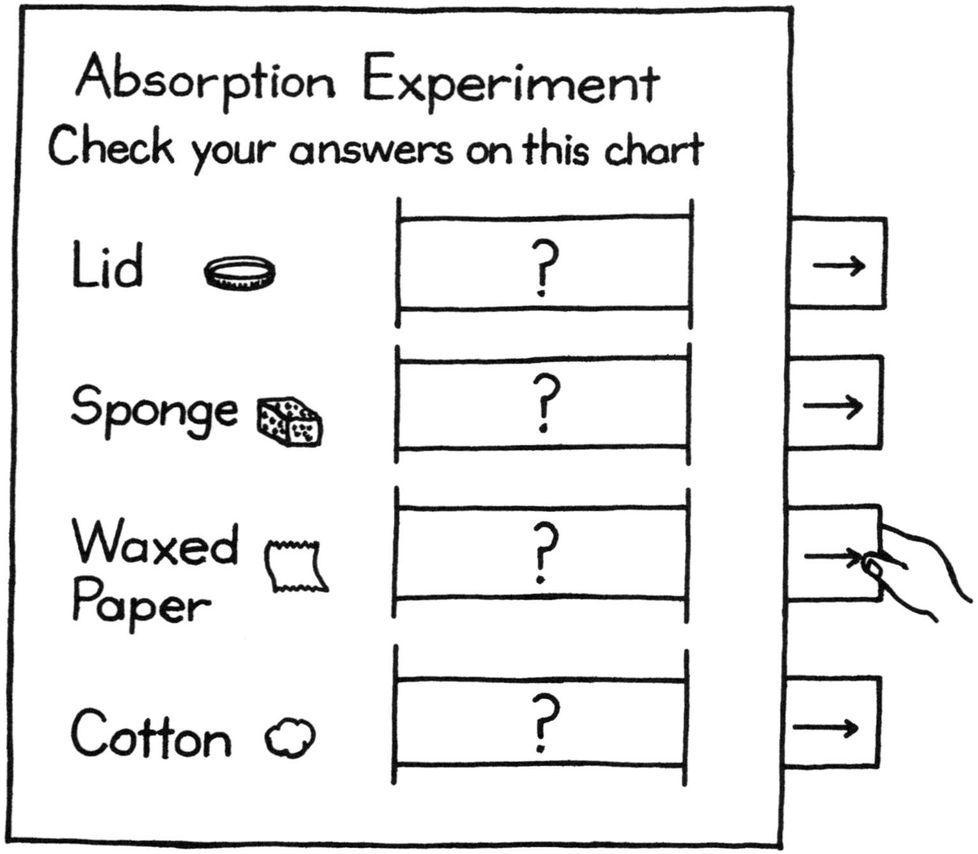

5

Check your answers on the chart.

Color-Mixing Experiment

You will need:

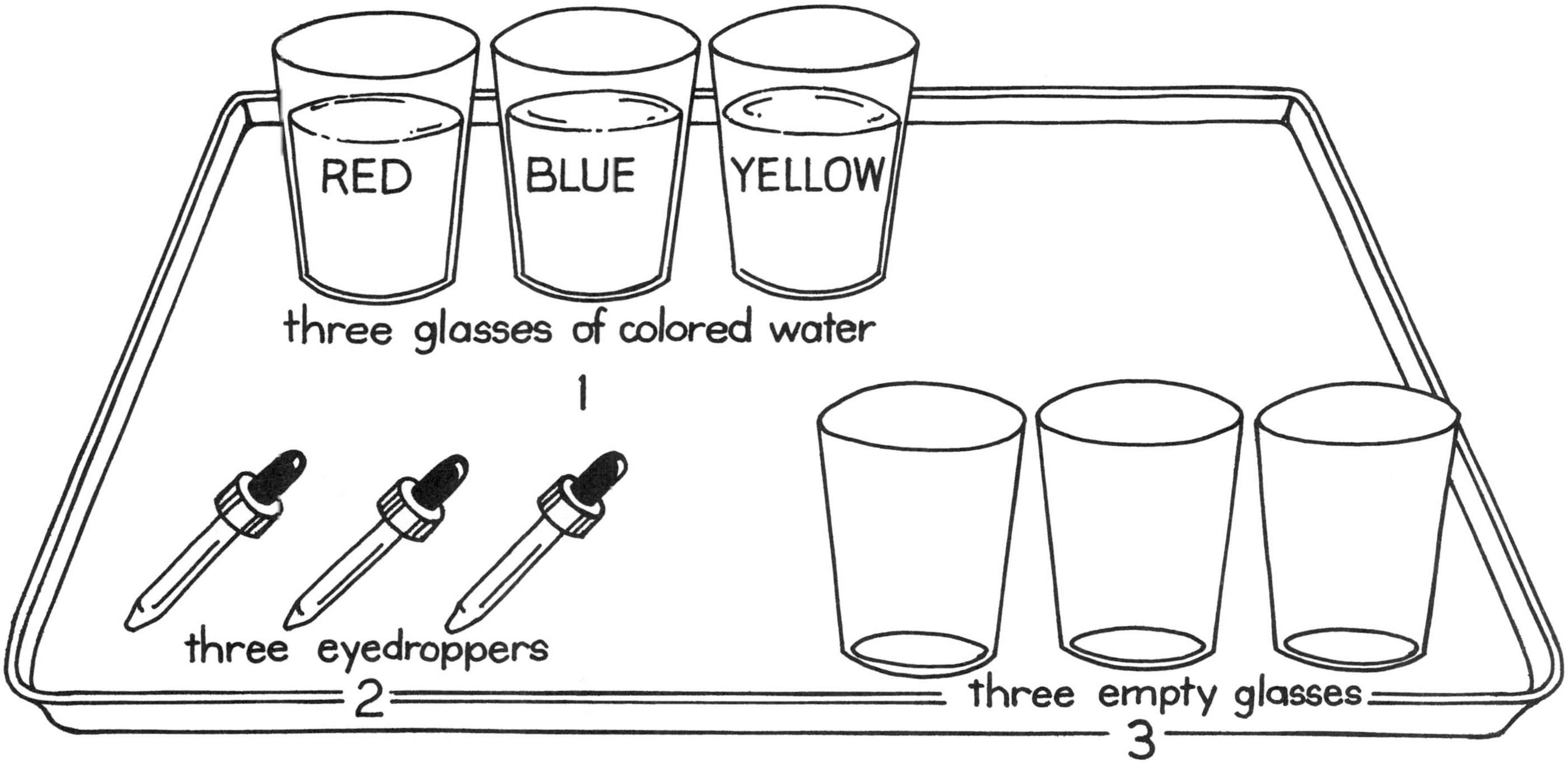

Color-Mixing Experiment

1

Add four drops of red.

2

Add four drops of blue.

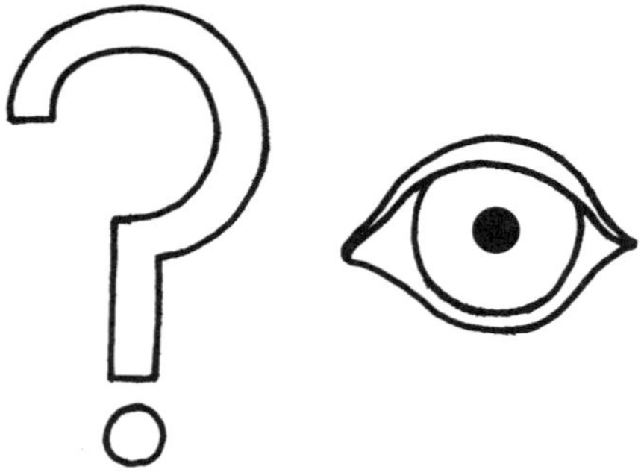

3

What color is it ?

4

Check your answer.

Color-Mixing Experiment

5

Add four drops of red.

6

Add four drops of yellow.

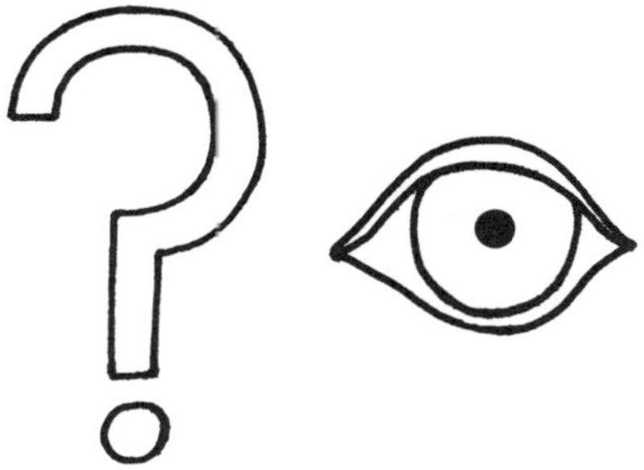

7

What color is it ?

8

Check your answer.

Color-Mixing Experiment

9

Add four drops of yellow.

10

Add four drops of blue.

11

What color is it ?

12

Check your answer.

Float-or-Sink Experiment

You will need:

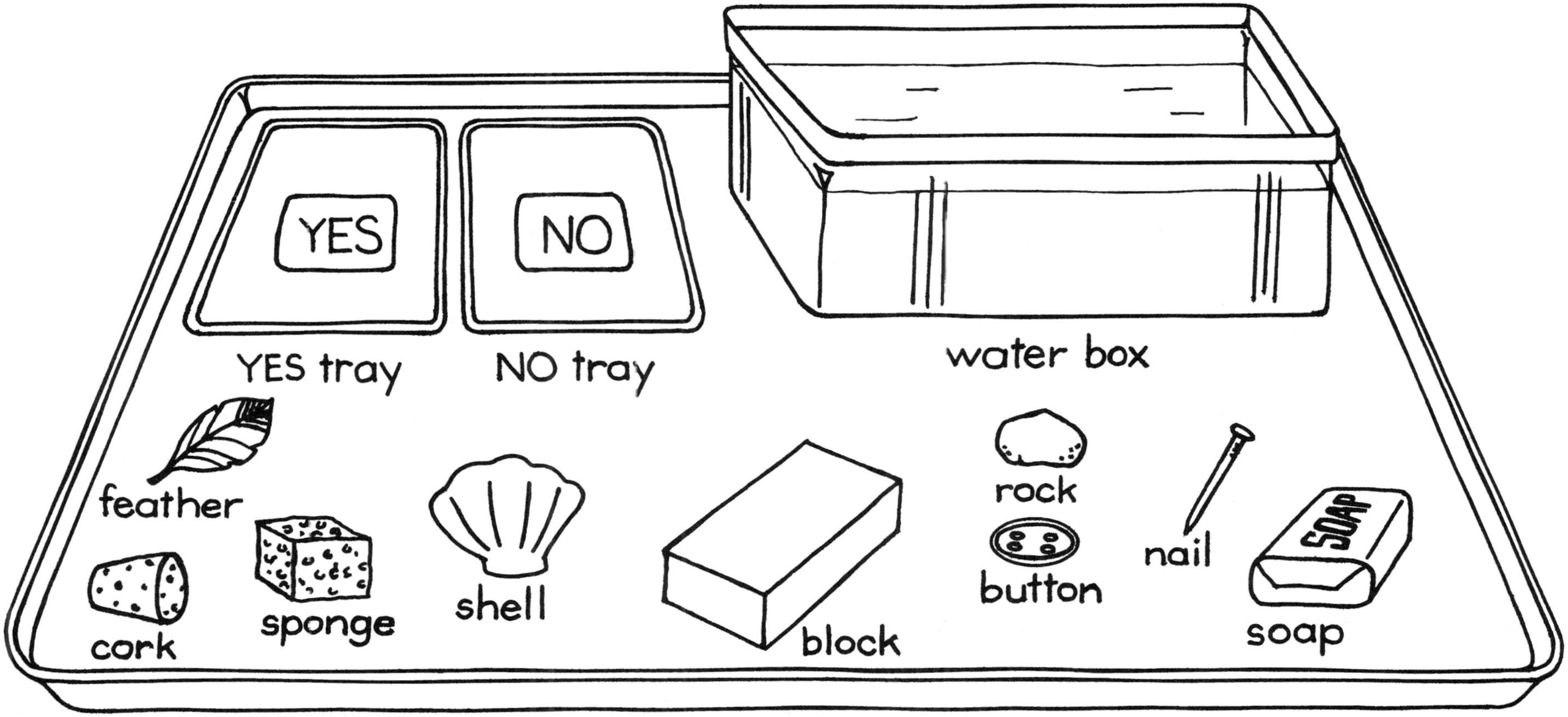

Float-or-Sink Experiment

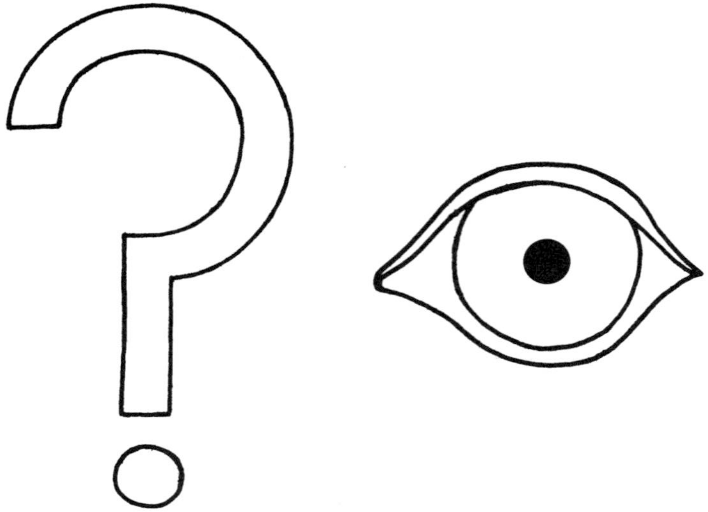

1

Look at the items. Which ones will float?

2

Put items on the YES tray or the NO tray.

Float-or-Sink Experiment

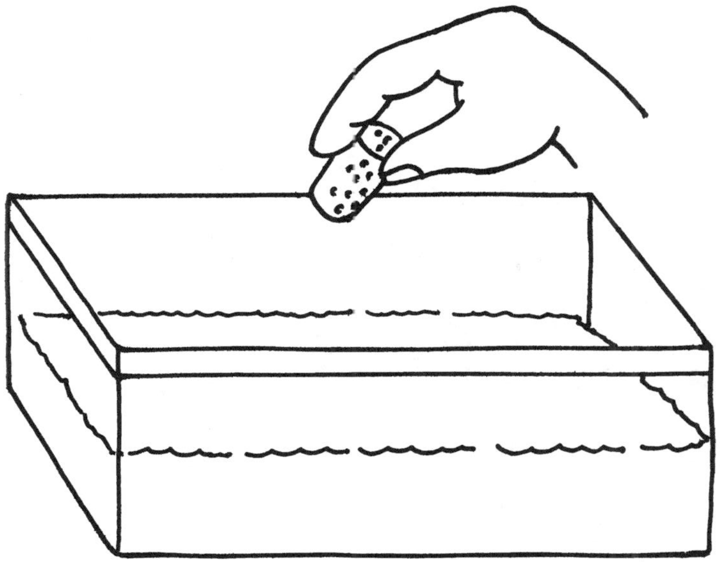

3

Try to float the items.

4

Put items that float on the YES tray. Put others on the NO tray.

Will It Attract?

You will need:

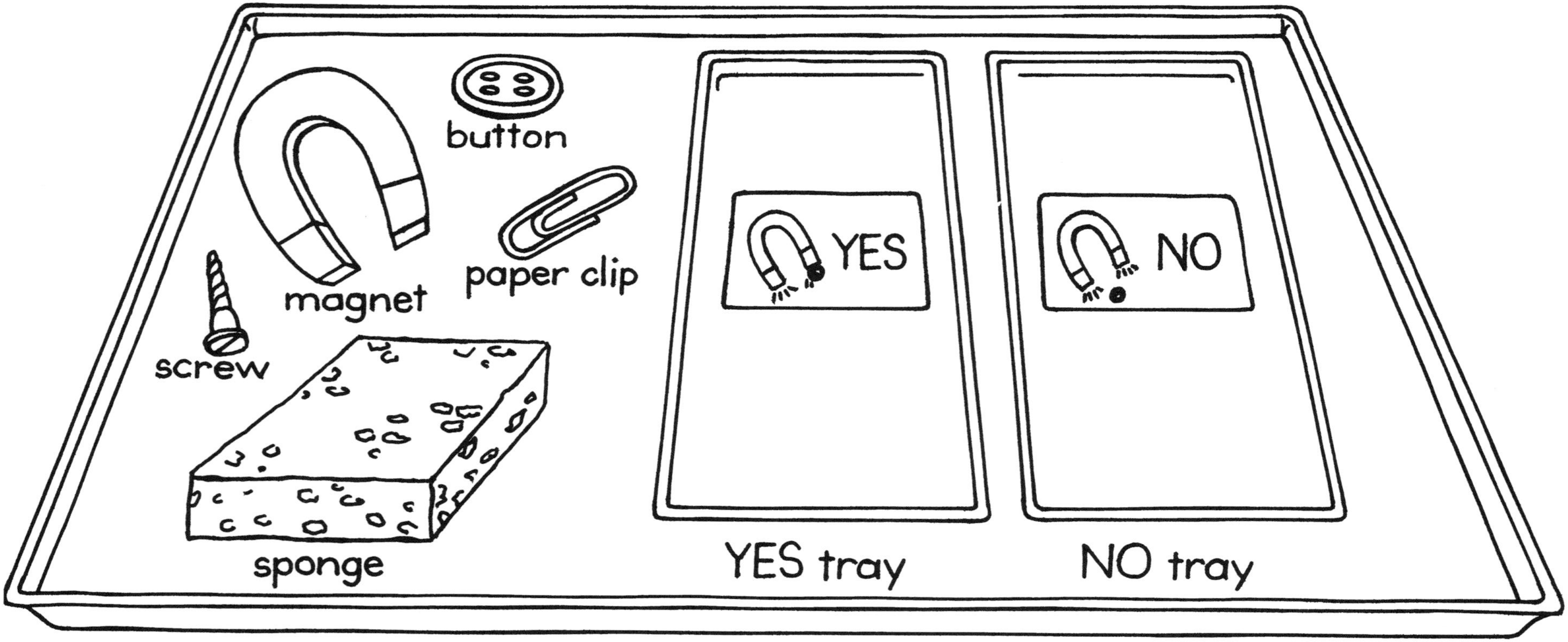

Will It Attract?

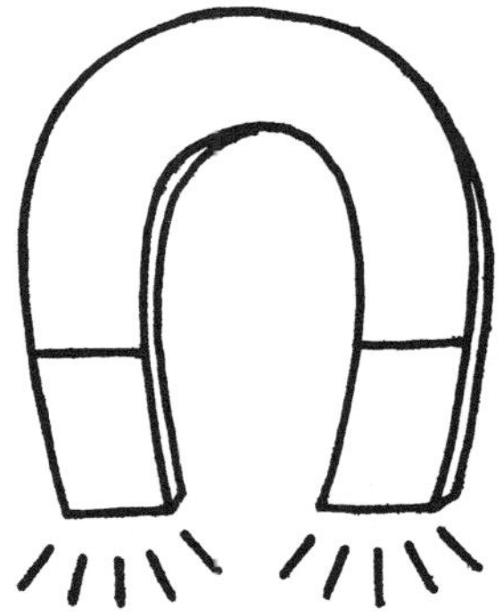

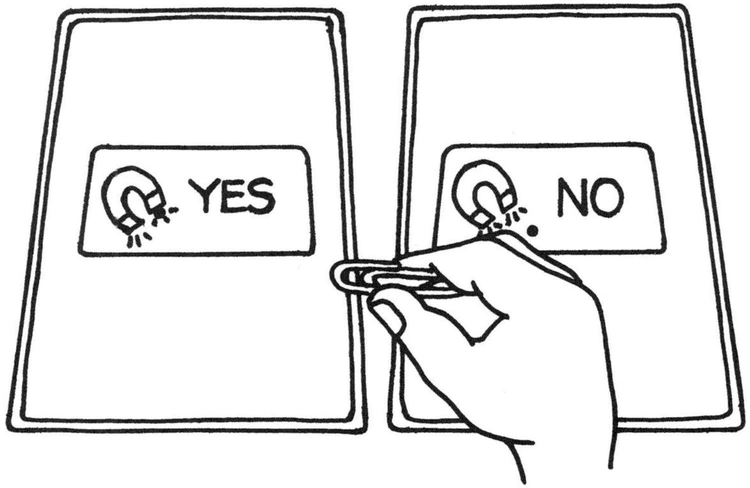

1

Look at the items. Which ones will attract?

2

Put the items that will attract on the YES tray. Put others on the NO tray.

Will It Attract?

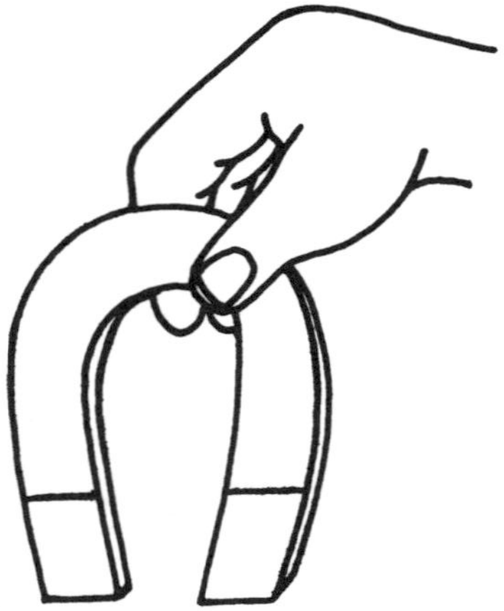

3

Use the magnet
Which items does it
attract?

4

Put items that attract
on the YES tray. Put
others on the NO tray.

Ingredients

lemons or
lemon juice

lettuce

apple

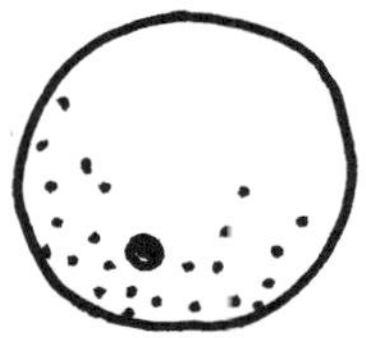
orange

tomato

onion

cheese

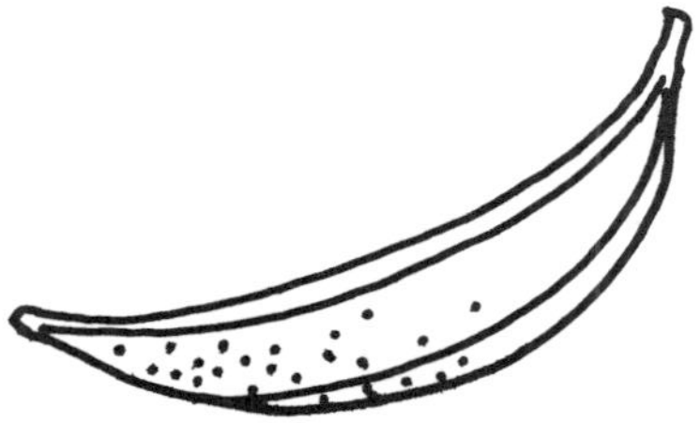
banana

bread

cornmeal

pear

peach

Ingredients

vanilla

spices

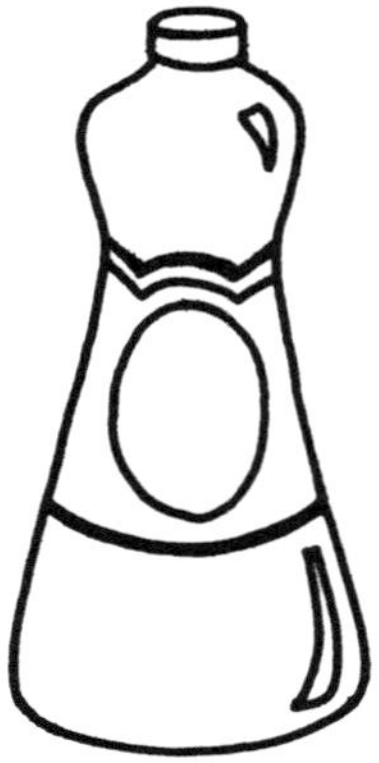

cooking oil

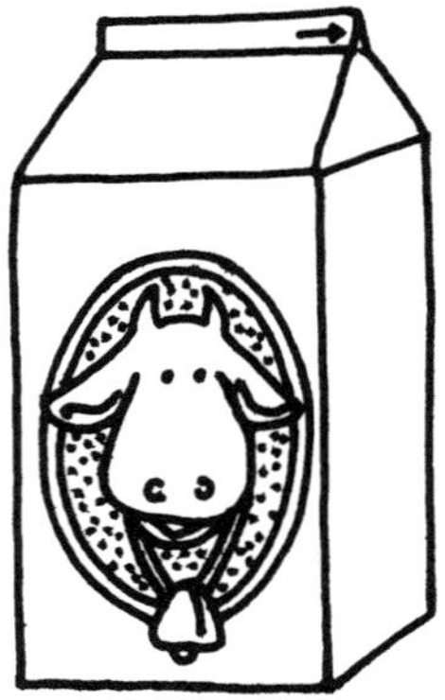

milk

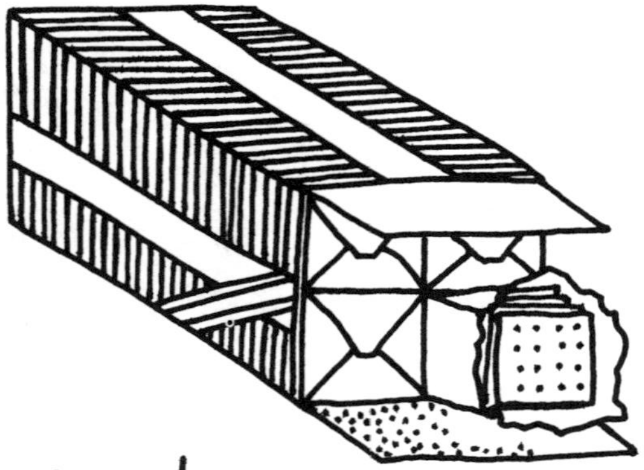

crackers

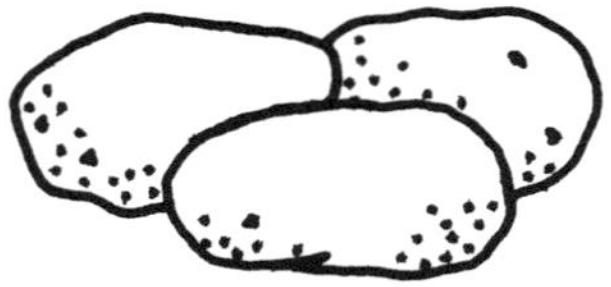

potatoes

carrots

Ingredients

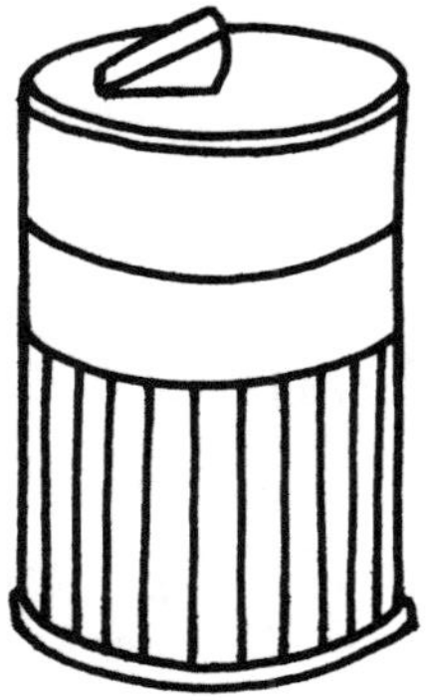

salt

sugar

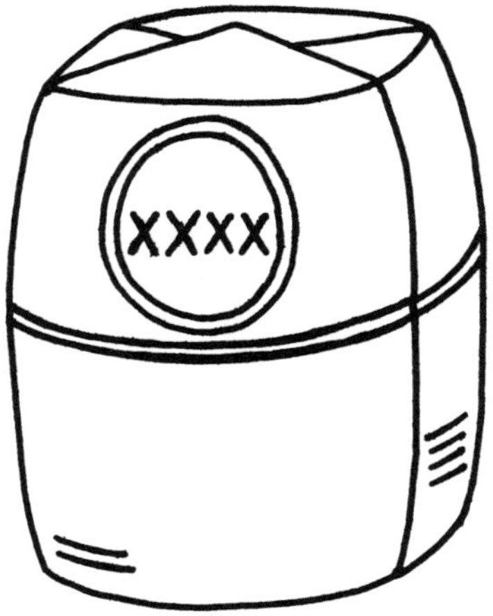

flour

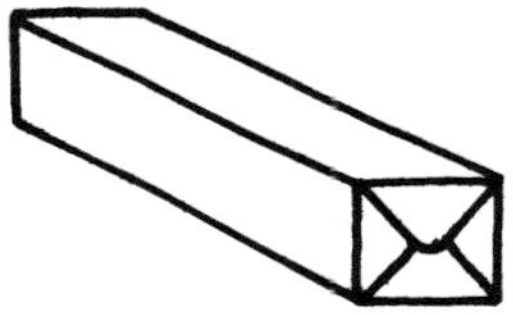

margarine

eggs

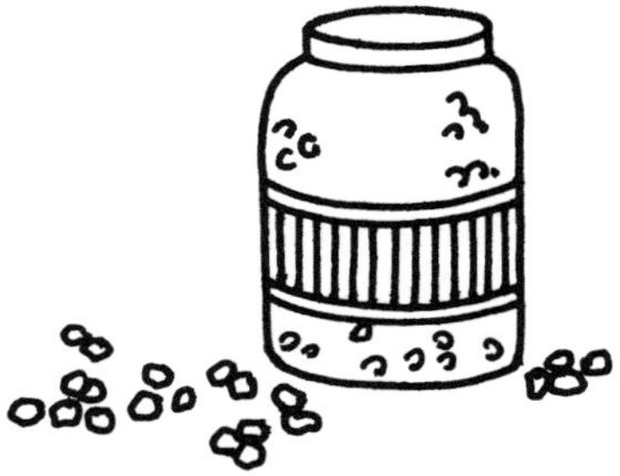

popcorn

Ingredients

celery

baking powder

baking soda

shortening

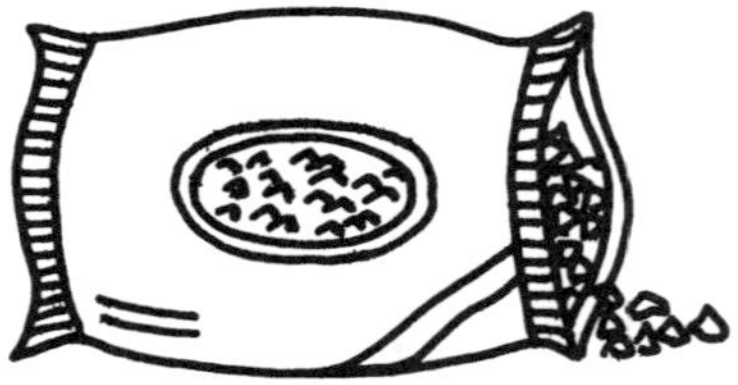

chocolate chips

powdered sugar

brown sugar

coconut

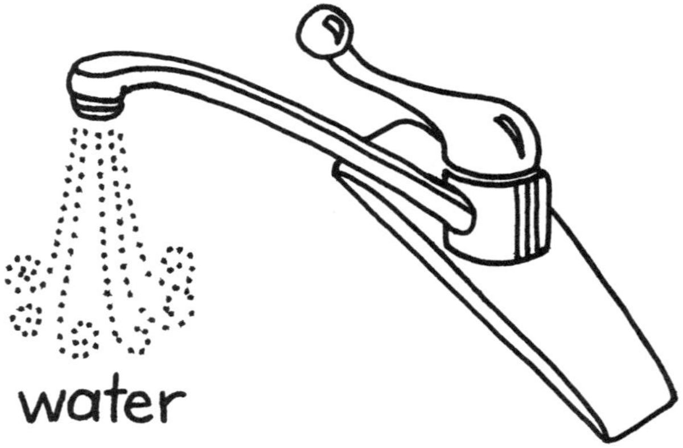

water

Utensils

baking pan
knife
chopper
hot plate
funnel
blender
ladle
egg whip
baking sheet or bread board
fork
pie plate

Utensils

1C
3/4
1/2
1/4
2/3
1/3
liquid measuring cup
bowl
spoon
tablespoon
teaspoon
½ teaspoon
¼ teaspoon
masher
strainer
spatula
rotary beater
1 CUP
½ CUP
⅓ CUP
1 cup
½ cup
⅓ cup
¼ cup
dry-ingredient measuring cups
turner

Processes

grate

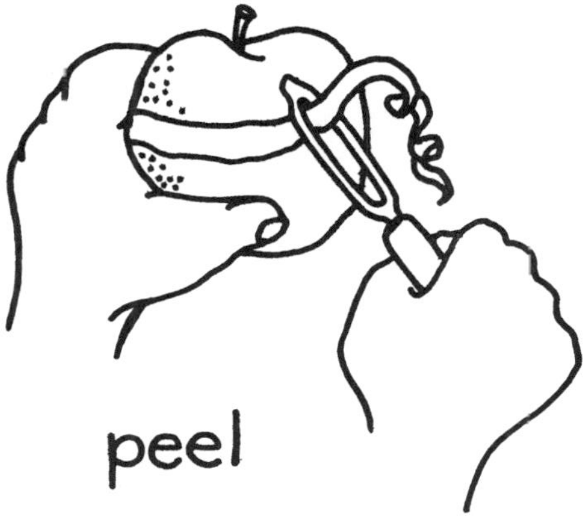

peel

grease

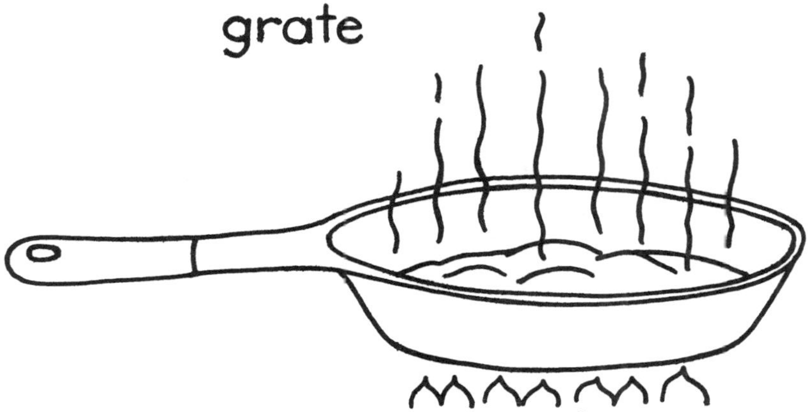

fry

pinch

Processes

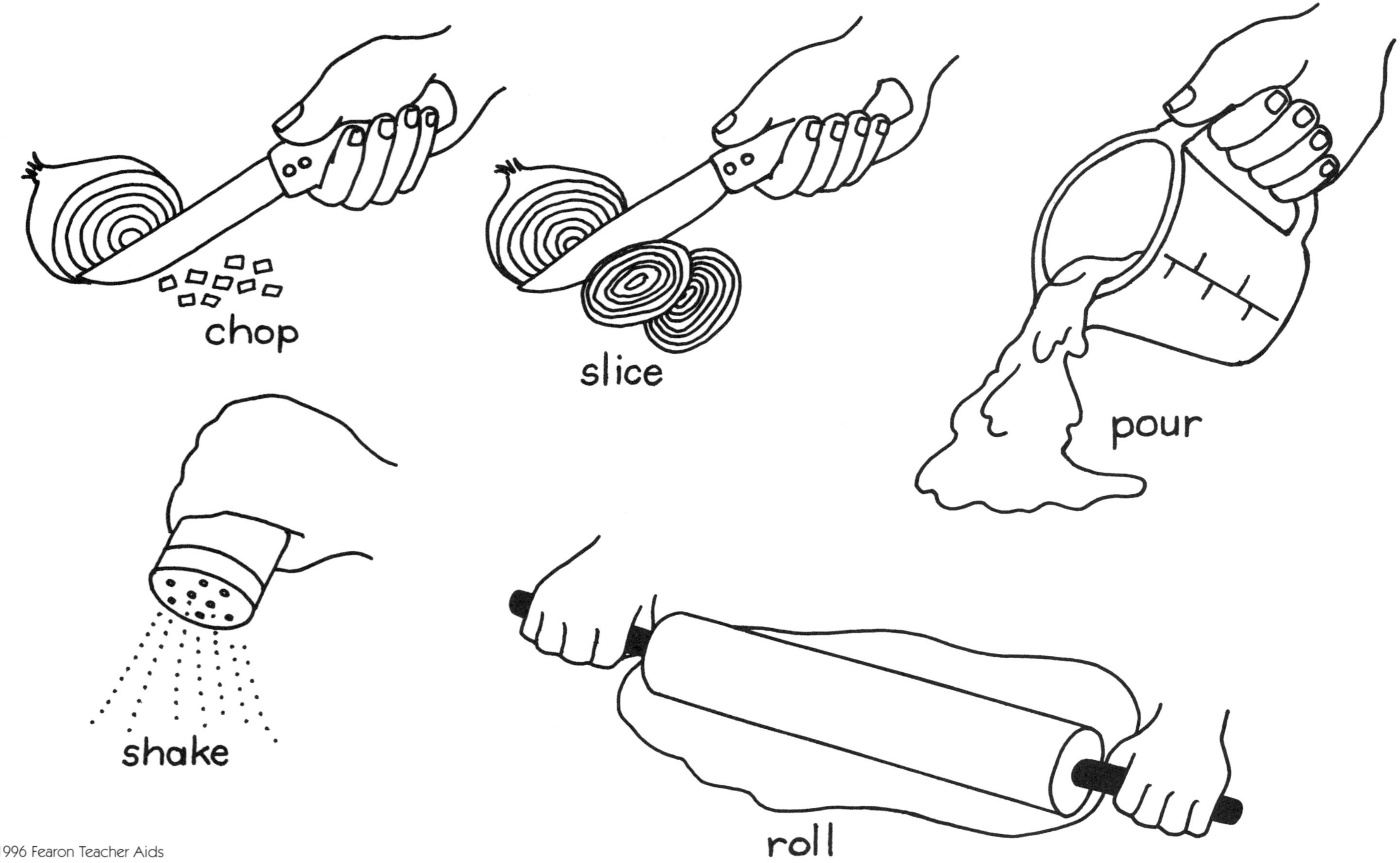

Spring Salad

You will need:

radishes

carrots

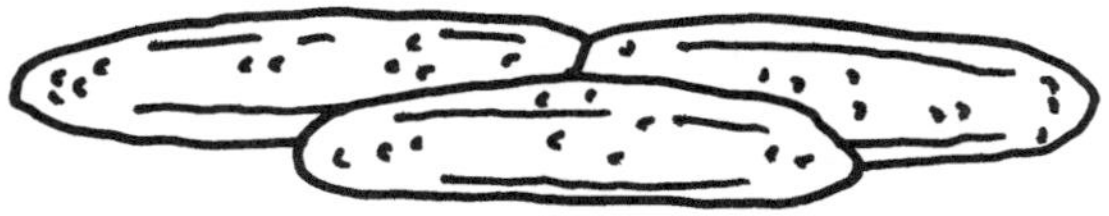
cucumbers

spinach or

lettuce

large bowl

vegetable peeler

vegetable brush

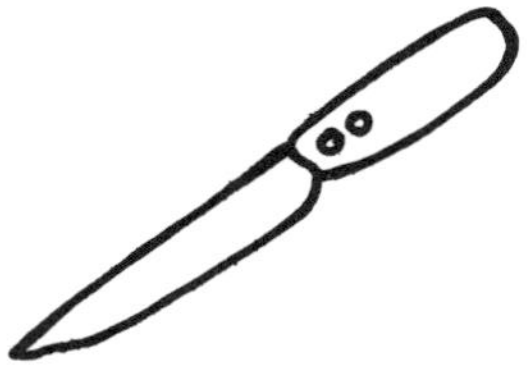
knife

Spring Salad

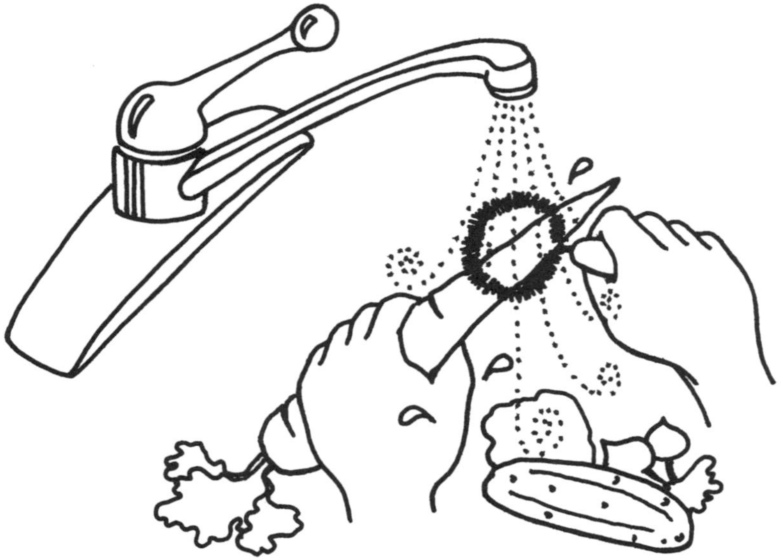

1

Scrub the vegetables.

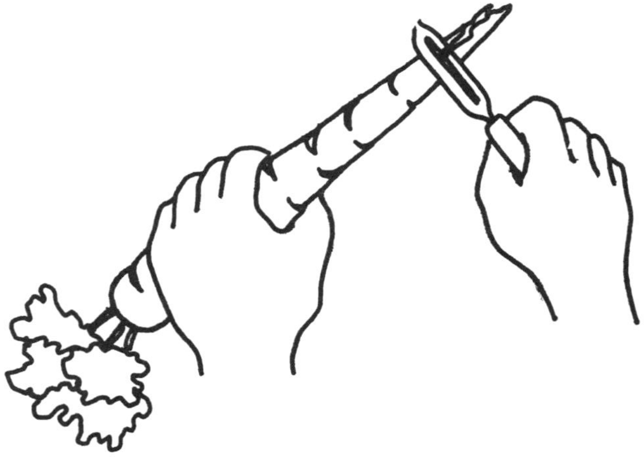

2

Peel the carrots.

Spring Salad

3

Slice the radishes, cucumbers, and carrots.

4

Tear the spinach or lettuce.

Spring Salad

5

Mix

6

Serve and eat the salad.

Easy Cookies

You will need:

2 sticks
margarine

1 cup flour

1 teaspoon
baking soda

1 cup brown sugar

2 cups oatmeal

large bowl

baking sheet

measuring cup

teaspoon

Easy Cookies

1

Put all ingredients in a bowl.

2

Mix with your hands.

Easy Cookies

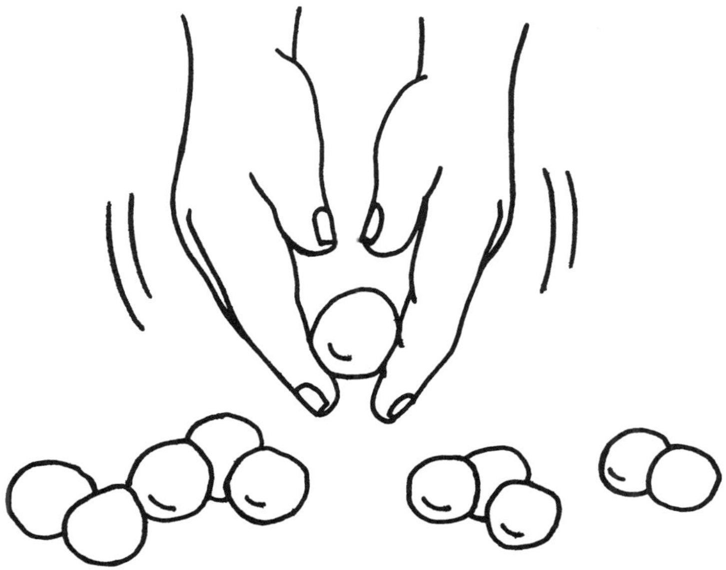

3

Roll dough into
1-inch balls.

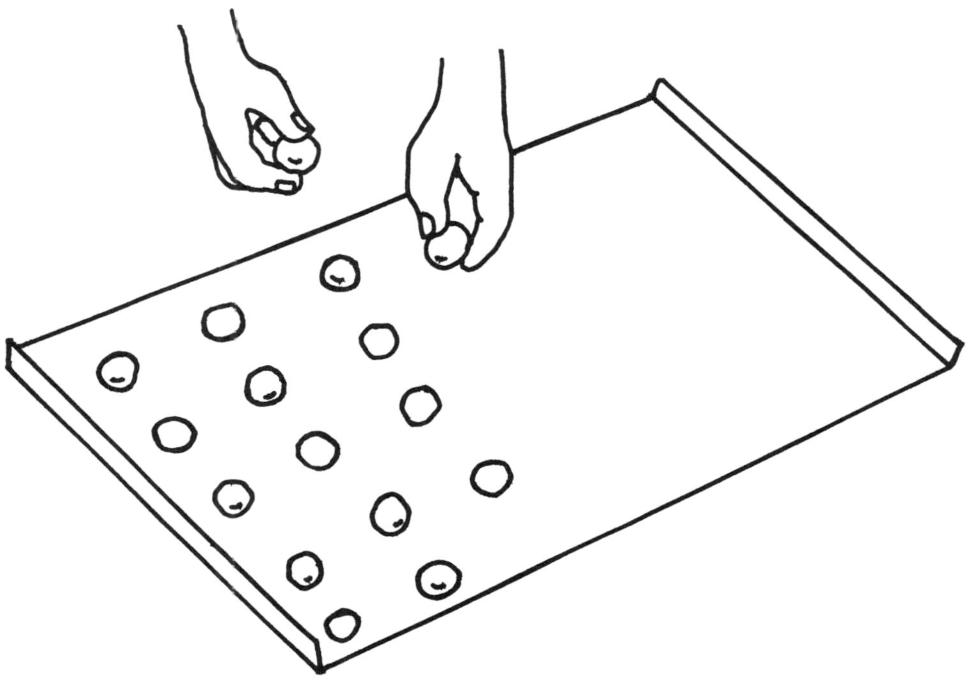

4

Put dough balls on a
baking sheet.

Easy Cookies

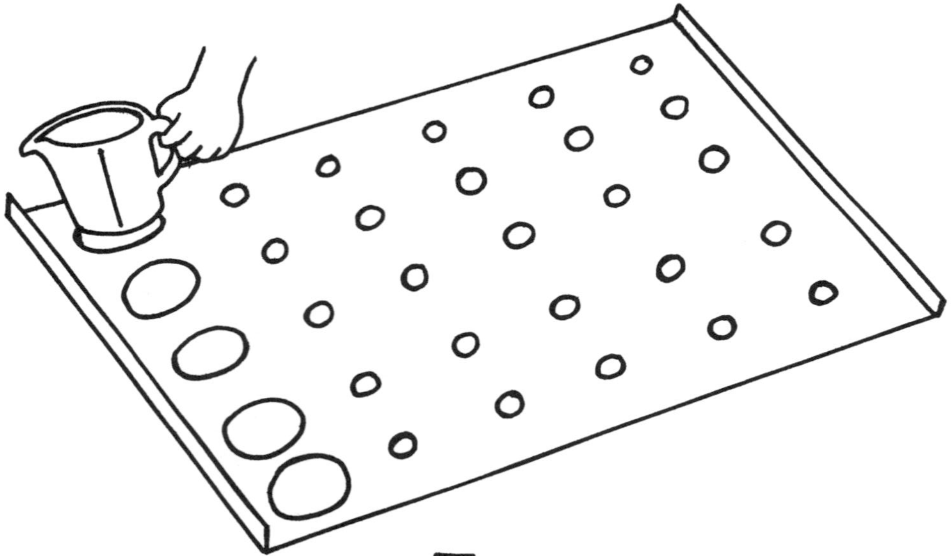

5

Flatten the balls with a measuring cup.

6

Bake cookies in a 350°F oven for 10 minutes.

Pineapple-Cheese Spread On Crackers With Milk

You will need:

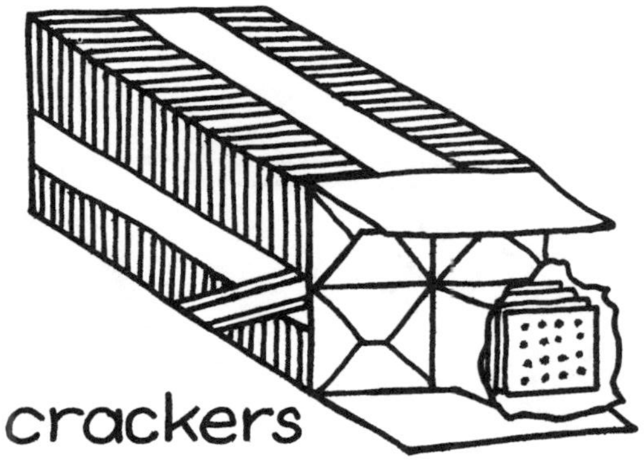
crackers

pineapple-cheese spread

milk

cutting board

knife

pitcher

glasses

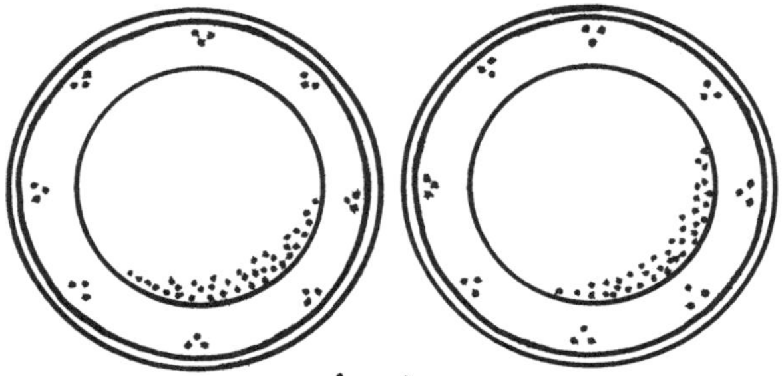
plates

Pineapple-Cheese Spread On Crackers With Milk

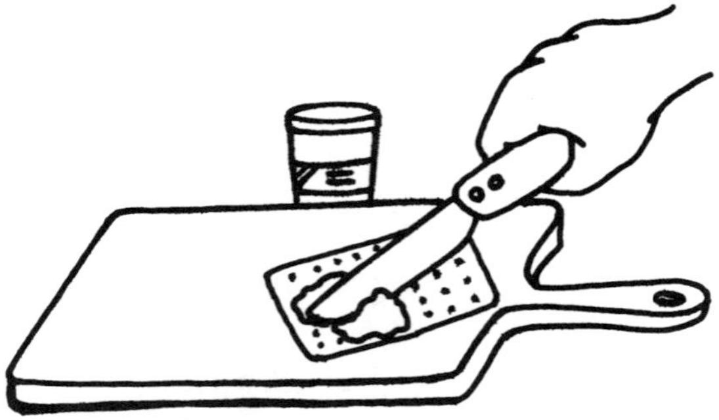

1

Spread cheese on crackers.

2

Put crackers on a plate.

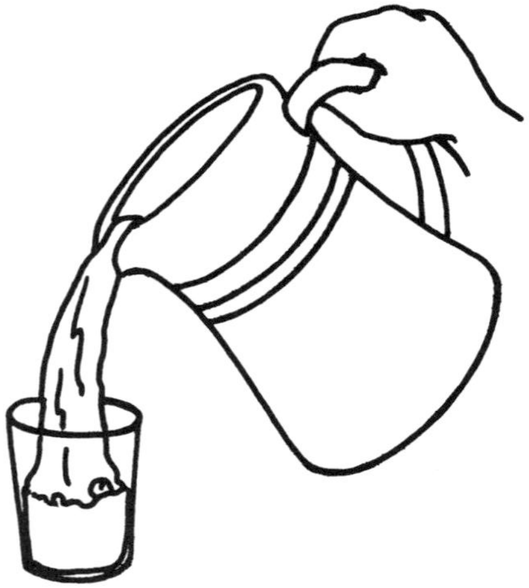

3

Pour milk into glasses.

Apples and Cheese

You will need:

apple

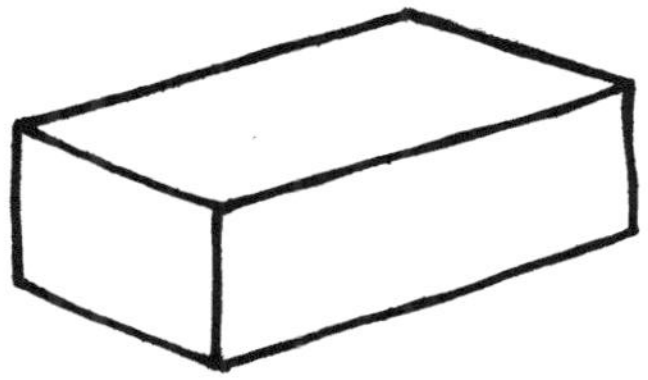

cheese

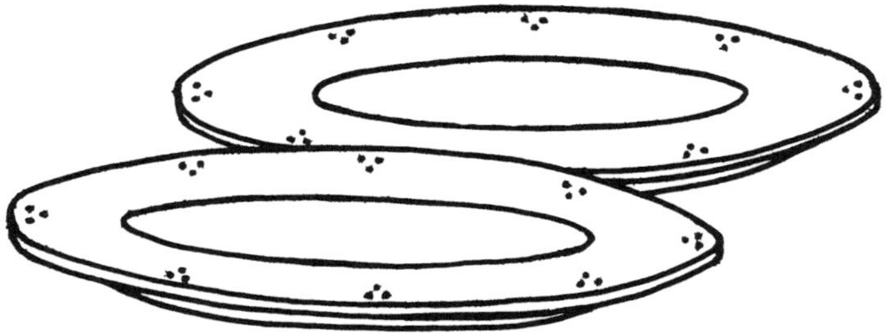

plates

knife

toothpicks

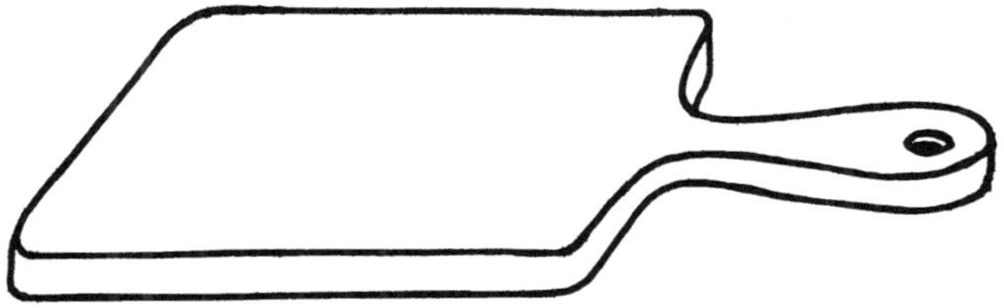

cutting board

Apples and Cheese

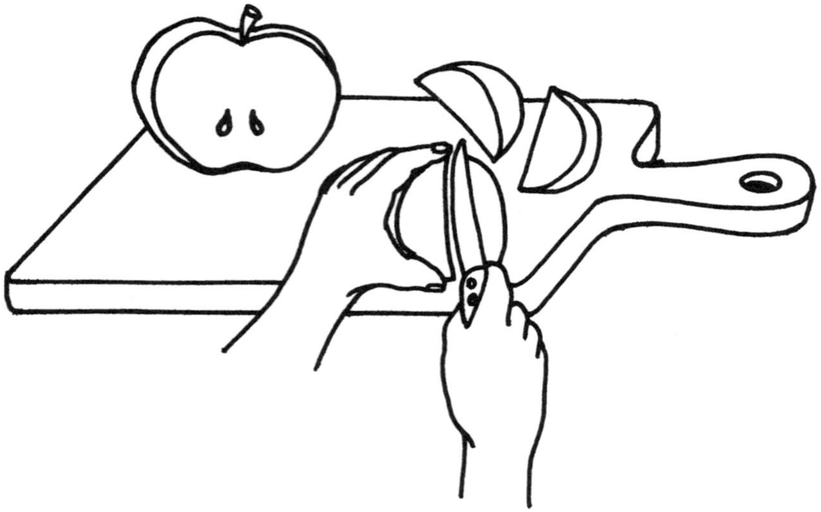

1

Cut apple into wedges.

2

Cut cheese into cubes.

Apples and Cheese

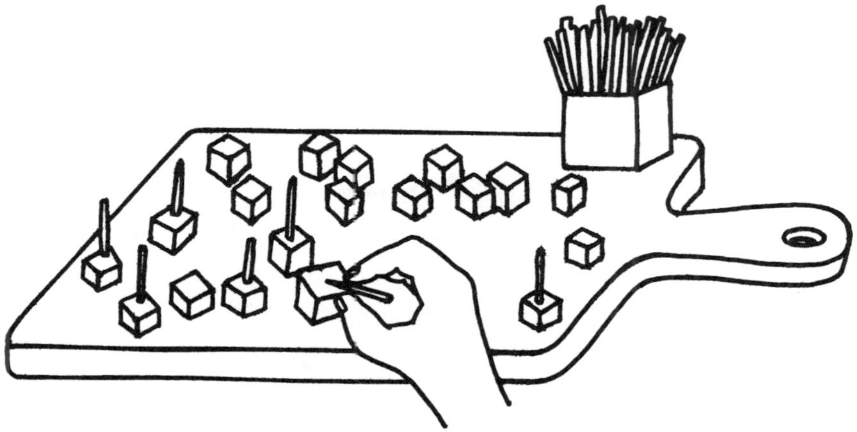

3

Put toothpicks in cheese.

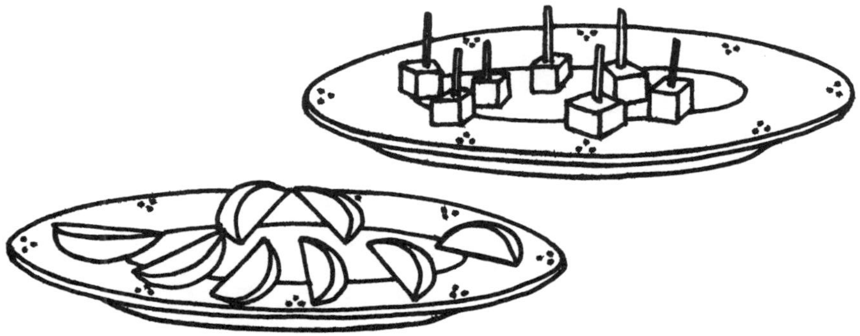

4

Put apples and cheese on plates.

Beanbag Toss

1

Get beanbags from the box.

2

Stand behind the line to toss the beanbags.

3

Return the beanbags to the box.

3

Classroom Cues and Markers

Color or picture cues in learning centers help guide children's behavior with minimal verbal instruction from you. One of the best ways to determine which cues to use is through observation. Children may be using the materials well as it is so they don't need cues. Or they may need help in knowing how to use materials or in putting them away.

When children become accustomed to using cues, they develop a respect for organization and equipment. Young children can use cues to find things without adult assistance. That frees you to interact with them in more positive, purposeful ways.

A room that emphasizes self-direction and indirect guidance makes use of many cueing systems. All the patterns in this book are variations of cues that can be used as

- center markers
- shelf indicators
- music cues
- cueing picture files and music files
- helping charts
- planning charts
- symbol charts
- rebus charts
- rebus stories

This chapter offers suggestions for making and using some of these cues in centers.

Interest Center Markers

Center markers are pictorial signs that show the activity that will occur in a particular area of the room or playground.

Print the name of the center using manuscript lettering; make the signs multilingual if many children speak second languages.

Color cue center markers to the planning board indicators so children can coordinate their plans for the day with the various centers available. (Refer to Chapter 5, planning boards.)

Mark interest centers with any of the following:

- a sign
- a mobile
- a poster
- a wall hanging

Signs and Posters

Signs can be simple, but they must be clear. Include a drawing or picture that describes the activities and include the name of the center in manuscript printing. Children will associate the activities of each center with the drawing or picture and the corresponding words.

A poster is generally more complex than a sign. It may be larger and include more detail. A poster would include the name of the interest center, and it would show pictures or drawings of activities in that center. You can use photographs of children playing in the center. Actual objects will make the poster three-dimensional. For example, include a puppet or a flannel-board figure on the Language Arts Center poster. A rock or a shell could add interest to the Discovery Center poster. Include doll house furniture on the Dramatic Play Center poster. Include a label in a second language if applicable.

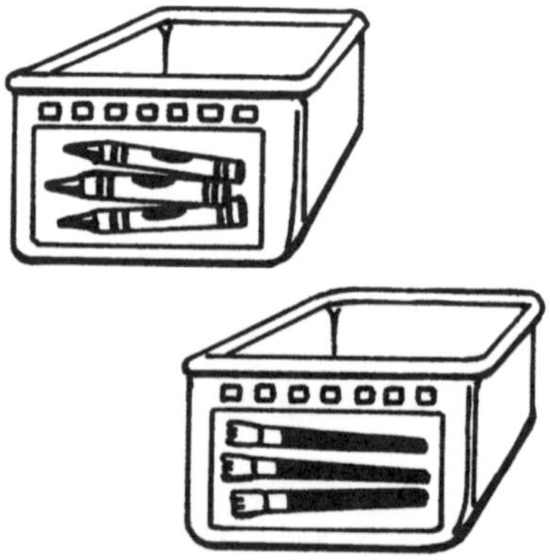

Mobiles

Mobiles are an excellent way to mark centers. To avoid a cluttered look, keep designs simple and straightforward. Use a mobile to mark those interest centers that are available only occasionally; hanging the mobile announces that the center is open. Hang the water play mobile near the water table when it's available or hang a mobile depicting a trip near the door if you have a field trip planned for that day.

The following suggestions and illustrations offer some ideas.

- Use well-executed manuscript printing for mobiles.
- Children should be able to view illustrations or objects from all sides of the mobile.
- Hang mobiles low so children can view them easily.
- Rotate mobiles to maintain interest.

Wall Hangings

Use wall hangings made by the children in some of your centers. To make a wall hanging, make pocket hems at the top and bottom of a piece of burlap or other fabric and thread a dowel though the hems. Fasten a cord to hang the fabric from the wall. Attach objects or drawings to the fabric with staples or stitches. Children can make a mural for a center from an old sheet. Put the sheet on a table and let the children use non-toxic felt-tip markers to decorate with illustrations related to the center. Go over the drawings with a permanent marker to make them washable. (Children should not use permanent markers because they are toxic.)

Canopies and Dropped Ceilings

Create an enclosure for the library, dramatic play area, or "alone space" with a tent-like structure or a canopy. To create this enclosure, suspend fabric squares or strips on dowels hung from the ceiling. Add a sign and pictures to show the name of the center.

Children's artwork may provide another type of ceiling cue. Children who are in the representational stage of art (about five years old) can draw a picture of the center. Mount the artwork on cardboard, then punch holes in all four corners of the drawing and suspend it from the ceiling. Finish by adding the name of the center.

You can make an interesting dropped-ceiling "sky" from an old blue sheet or a piece of blue fabric. Pin cutouts of planets, sun, and stars to the fabric and suspend it from string tied to all four corners.

Illustrations as Cues

Cut out magazine pictures of learning center items from catalogs or magazines, laminate, and cover with clear vinyl. Fasten them securely to the shelf or to the rise of the shelf. This method works particularly well for unit blocks. For younger children, cues need to be the exact size of the blocks or other objects. Place them on shelf surfaces so you can store the blocks or other objects directly on top of them. Everything should be on one level. For older children, cues can be smaller representations of the objects. The block rebus chart in Chapter 2 shows children how to use these types of cues.

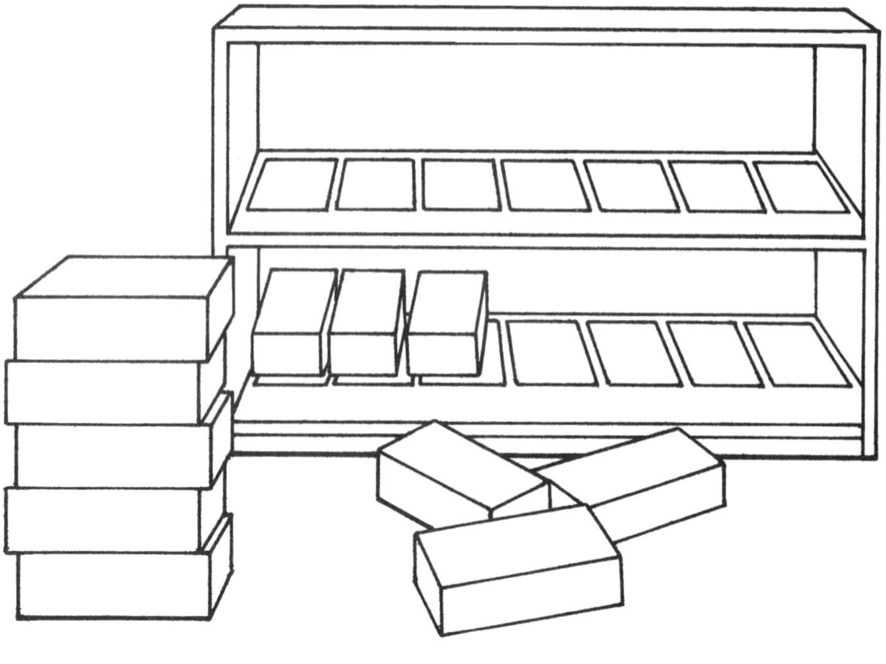

Codes as Cues

Use colored dots to show the correct placement of objects. For example, a dot on a shelf can show the placement of block props or rhythm instruments. Teach children that items belong on shelves with corresponding dots.

Diagrams as Cues

Use general diagrams with older children to represent an area of the classroom. This type of exercise reinforces map, chart, and graph-reading skills. You can use charts and diagrams to illustrate an obstacle course, show where rest mats belong, or how children should park tricycles in the parking lot. Position charts where children can easily see them. Spend some time explaining them to individual children who are ready for the concept. If they don't understand, they may simply not be ready for this idea. Children who do understand will teach other children.

Storage Cues

Use storage cues in only one or two areas of the classroom at a time so children can gradually become accustomed to the idea. Start by marking the storage places for only a few items in an area. Point out these cues to children. Make sure they understand what the cues mean. When you introduce new materials to the classroom, make cues for them and show these to children.

Include printed words on the cues to encourage association between words and the objects they represent. Many children will learn these words as their first reading vocabulary. Again, use a second language if appropriate.

If you use individual cues, laminate them or cover them with adhesive-backed transparent vinyl so they will last longer.

Finally, let children help you cue shelves; they'll not only feel greater ownership for the classroom and materials this way, but will also be better able to teach other children where things belong.

You can choose from a variety of methods to cue shelves. Here are some suggestions:

Draw the cues as simple outlines on non-stick paper before you line shelves. This type of cueing works particularly well for table games because this center gets changed frequently. Double the paper before placing it on shelves so you can turn it over and use it again.

Use trays, box lids, rectangular baking pans, or plastic refrigerator containers to store individual projects. Draw the outlines of objects to be stored directly on the tray or on liners cut to fit the tray. This system works well in the Creative Art Center and in the Discovery Center. For example, use and store all the items for a Float-or-Sink activity on a tray. To protect against moisture, use a permanent marking pen and laminate or cover the cue with clear vinyl.

To show children where to hang items on a peg board, screen, or bulletin board, trace outlines of objects on mural paper where they should be hung up. Attach outline to peg board before adding hooks. Make sure hooks match the correct pictures of objects.

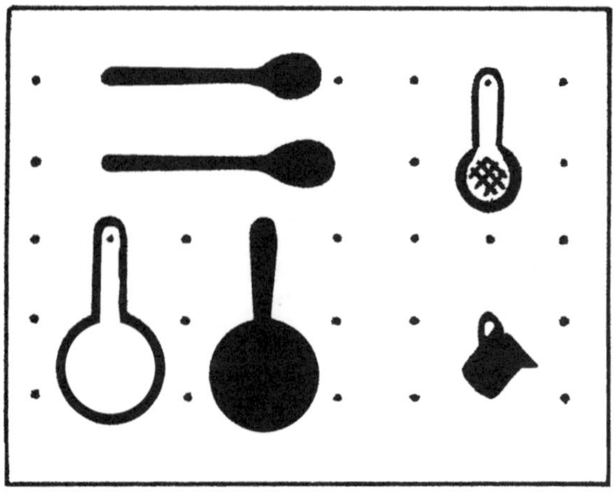

Music Cues

Use cueing as a teaching aid. For example, children can learn to use the tape recorder and play the piano by following rebuses and picture cues. They can play simple songs by following a color-coded song. Include songs from children's second languages where necessary. Cue tone bells, xylophones, and xylopipes in a similar way. Place song cues on a strip of poster board that is approximately 36" long and 8" high. Place "music" on a music stand so that the children can see several measures of a song at a time and play it by themselves. One line on a page works better than a top-to-bottom sequence; children have a hard time keeping their place when they must look from the keyboard back to the music.

Children love to use tape recorders and record players. Cue the *on* buttons with a green piece of tape and the *off* buttons with a red piece of tape. Mark *rewind*, *fast forward*, and the direction in which to move the record player arm with arrows.

Meet with small groups of children to talk about how to use equipment. Gather a box of records and tapes that the children can use. "Teacher only" records and tapes can be kept on a high storage shelf.

Use the tape recorder.

1. Push ● to start.
2. Push ● to stop.
3. Push ● to rewind.

Chapter Checklist

	Yes	No
1. Have I observed children in my group to see where cueing would be helpful and appropriate?		
2. Have I marked my learning centers with a center sign or a mobile?		
3. Do my center signs have pictures of the kinds of activities in which children can engage in that center and the name of the center in correct manuscript print?		
4. Have I used real objects for young children and realistic pictures for older children?		
5. Are storage spaces cued so children will know what goes where when they are finished with materials or when it is clean-up time?		
6. Are tape recorders and other machines cued so that children can use them with a minimum of adult assistance?		
7. Have I increased the difficulty of my cues starting with very concrete cues and progressing to slightly more difficult cues as children increase in their skills?		
8. Have I observed to see which cues are actually being "read" and which ones are ignored?		
9. Have I used my observations to make decisions about adding or deleting cues?		

Symbol and Rebus Charts

Making, Displaying, and Storing

Children process information in different ways. Twenty percent rely mostly on auditory cues, thirty percent use predominantly visual cues, and fifty percent use a combination of both. Most young children respond better to short, concise directions and directions illustrated with pictures and symbols.

When designing picture cues for children, start with basic symbols that represent everyday actions. For example, a picture of an eye suggests *see, look, observe,* or *notice*. The symbol of the mouth represents *speaking, talking,* or *responding*, and the tongue is the symbol for *taste*. Hands suggest *touching, feeling,* or *doing*. The question mark represents *thinking, questioning,* or *wondering*. Use these patterns as cues to suggest appropriate actions to the children.

General Symbols

Introducing Action Symbols

Make a set of symbols on small cards and carry them with you throughout the day. Use them instead of words to suggest specific actions to children, such as listening or cleaning up.

Use symbols to indicate the need for especially careful observation or questioning. For example, a large question mark displayed next to a science experiment will help arouse children's interest.

Add an eye-and-question symbol to the beginning of rebus charts. This will encourage children to *look* and *think* before doing what the rebus says.

This chapter will give you instructions for making this kind of display device.

Use manuscript printing to write words that correspond to rebus symbols. Point words out to children. Patterns for manuscript letters are at the end of this chapter.

If children use or understand a second language, print the appropriate words next to corresponding symbols.

When children recognize the action symbol and the representative word, add another word for the action along with the name of the object. For example, the picture of a hand could have the word *touch* on it. Later, substitute the words *do* or *feel*. Still later, add the word *hand*. This communicates that one symbol may represent more than one idea.

Use action symbols early in the year to simplify the transition to more complex pictorial representations like rebus charts and recipes.

Using Symbol Charts

Use symbol charts to get children's attention, emphasize a point, or suggest a sequence of events.

Introduce each symbol chart with a symbol story. Use two or three symbols together on one chart. The chart might say *look, think,* and *do*. Print the words along with the symbols. Add second-language words, too, where appropriate.

Include symbolic representations of *same* and *different* and say the words *same, not same,* and *different* to children frequently. Draw or show pictures of two similar items to suggest sameness and two unlike items to suggest differences.

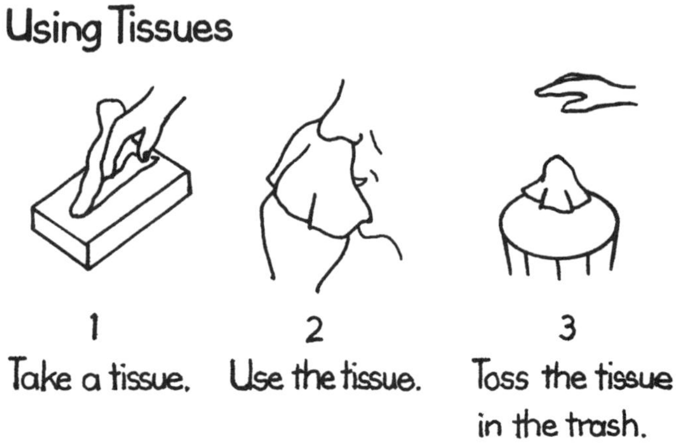

Charts can be used to help children make and check their predictions and hypotheses. Use symbols to represent the different steps in an activity or experiment.

In the example, below, children are exploring the concepts of magnetic and nonmagnetic. The sequence in a chart like this should always move from left to right. You would place this chart in the Discovery Center. On the table, provide a box of objects, a checking tray with a question mark to suggest questioning or wondering, a magnet, and an answer tray. Children remove an object from the box and predict whether or not it is magnetic. They check predictions by using a magnet, and indicate responses by placing objects in the answer tray. See Chapter 2 for more examples of checking charts.

Introducing Rebus Charts

Begin with rebus charts that include fewer than four pictures. Consider introducing charts with a single-step rebus such as *Put on a smock* or *Wash your hands*.(See the end of the chapter for samples.) As children become familiar with simple steps, they'll be ready to move to more complex charts. Gradually introduce other rebus charts for familiar routines. Chapter 9 contains many samples of rebus charts for routine activities.

After using simple rebuses for a while, gradually introduce longer charts for recipes and activities. Introduce each level of rebus chart slowly and give some explanation of the steps. When all of the children understand the sequence of various rebus charts, begin to use the rebuses with four and five steps and those that require left-to-right and up-and-down sequencing. Examples of rebus charts that use sequences are those shown in Chapter 2.

Using Rebus Charts

Once children have become accustomed to other kinds of symbol charts, introduce rebus signs into your daily routine. Rebuses are picture stories or messages that explain recipes, directions for activities, or instructions for using equipment. Once children learn to use rebuses, they become much more independent, self-directed learners.

Rebus charts also provide experience in the skill of left-to-right and top-to-bottom reading progression and, as such, are excellent early literacy tools. Although this type of "reading" is often based upon memorization and picture clues, children feel the thrill of making sense out of written messages.

Reading rebus charts also provides an excellent experience in following a specific sequence of events to achieve a desired result, as well as an opportunity to use memory skills in a meaningful way. Last, but certainly not least, rebus charts are fun. Children often think of them as puzzles to be solved.

Making Rebus Charts

Rebuses should follow a consistent format to be most effective. Here are some guidelines.

Charts should *always* be drawn in *left to right* and *top to bottom* sequence.

Drawings should represent the actual equipment that children will be using. For instance, the tape recorders in your classroom might need to be switched on in two places; make sure directions reflect this.

Drawings should clearly illustrate directions. Test for this by covering the words and looking at *only* the pictures and drawings as you try to do the process.

Use manuscript printing. Refer to the chart at the end of this chapter for print templates.

Add realistic color to the charts with felt-tip markers; use a variety of skin tones on figures of people.

Laminate the charts or cover with clear adhesive vinyl to reduce wear and tear.

The patterns for rebus charts included throughout this book provide basic symbols and drawings for producing many different types of rebus charts. You can use them as shown or adapt them to create original charts for your classroom. Some activities require more adult supervision than others do. The amount of supervision will depend on the individual class. Of course, children's safety should be a prime consideration. If an activity requires the use of hot or sharp instruments, you will want to be there to help.

Observe children using rebus charts. Note where difficulties occur and adjust charts accordingly. If children still have difficulty using the charts, think about providing a little more explanation or reviewing and rewriting classroom rules.

Lettering Rebus Charts

When designing rebus charts, use symbols that children can easily read. Although the charts will probably contain some printed words or numerals, the pictures must be the primary vehicle for conveying a message. This illustration is an example of an "incorrect" and a "correct" rebus.

Incorrect:

Correct:

The way you letter rebus charts is very important. The following principles are good guidelines for manuscript printing.

Varieties of letter styles can be confusing to young children. Try using the manuscript style illustrated at the end of this chapter.

Note that uppercase letters are a full line or space high, and most lowercase letters are only a half-space high. The lower-case *t* is the only letter that is three-fourths of a space in height. The lowercase *b, d, f, h, k,* and *l* are a full space high. Lowercase *g, j, p, q* and *y* are the only letters that extend below the main body of the letter.

Capitalize the first letter of a single-word caption or the first letter of the first word of a phrase. Print the remaining letters in lower-case letters. This style of capitalization is the accepted standard for textbooks and readers. Adoption of this form permits beginning readers to see the printed word as they do when they read.

Use the manuscript style of printing for all classroom materials including staff or parent bulletin boards. You may even want to alert parents to the style of lettering you use in the classroom so that they can use it at home.

Supplies for Making Rebuses

Gather construction supplies into a box with compartments like the inexpensive household caddy illustrated below. This type of container is usually available in the housewares department of variety stores.

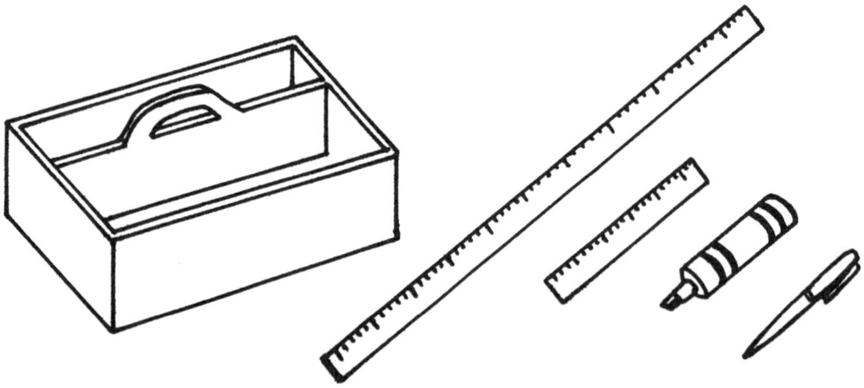

We recommend the following list of supplies for the projects contained in this book:

- a yard or meter stick
- a one-foot ruler
- water soluble felt-tip markers in basic colors; Marker tips should be approximately one-fourth of an inch wide to make broad marks for drawing and lettering.
- a black nylon-tip pen or marker

- oil-base (permanent) felt-tip markers in basic colors
- sharpened No. 2 pencils
- art gum eraser
- high-quality scissors. If possible, use a paper cutter for sheets of poster board. If you don't have access to a paper cutter, then take time to draw lightly penciled guidelines before cutting with scissors
- rubber cement
- a utility knife with interchangeable blades
- poster board
- tag board, a heavy paper available in 9" x 12" and 18" x 24" sizes, available in a variety of colors.

DISPLAYING CHARTS

he following suggestions will help you tailor the display and storage of ebus charts to your own teaching situation.

Always display steps or symbols in left-to-right order to reflect the way children will read. Use top-to-bottom sequence later.

Begin by taping two or three symbols on the table or tray where children use them. Attach the symbols to trays with circles of masking tape. Place the signs and materials on one level so that children can follow them visually. Children will have the symbols nearby so that they can easily refer to the cards. If possible, laminate the cards or cover them with clear vinyl.

Use tape or pushpins to attach individual cards or small charts to the wall; use chalkboards or easels for larger charts. Also try tacking charts to a bulletin board or punching holes in the top and hanging them from pegboard hooks. Use sturdy window shades in close proximity to center areas for displaying charts.

Make slot charts. Purchase them at school-supply stores or make them from heavy cardboard. Cut slits horizontally into poster board and staple or tape the openings around the bottom and sides. Slip charts into the slots.

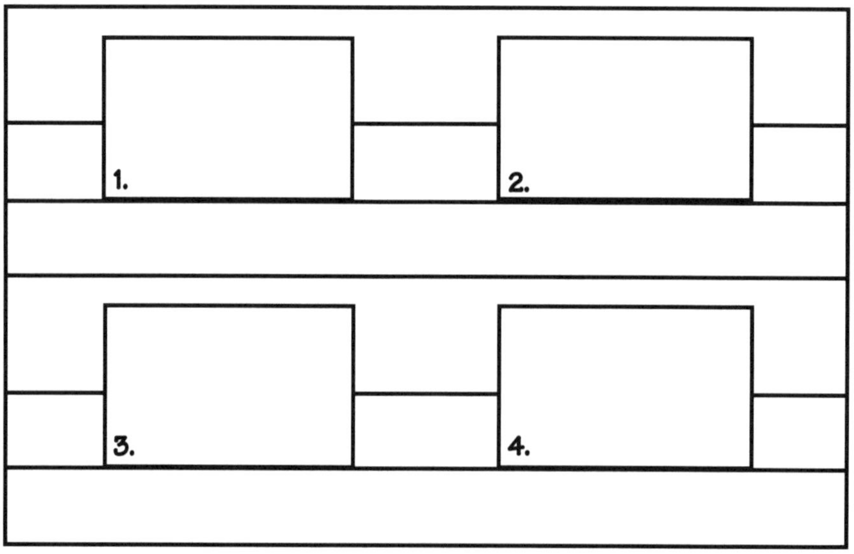

Make your own chartholders. First, pour plaster into a spray can lid and immediately insert a plastic clothes clip with the open end up. Let dry. (If you use a pinch-type clothespin, wrap a rubber band around the ends so that the clothespin is slightly open when you insert it into the plaster.) To display charts, insert them into clothespins. Use two holders for larger charts.

Make a freestanding triangular display board from three sides of a heavy cardboard box. First, cut out three sections of the box along the corner creases. Fold the creases to form a triangular shape. Fasten down the sides with a staple gun or strong tape, then tape or staple tag board strips to the box at the desired intervals. Besides acting as a display board for rebus charts, this box can serve as a roof in the Block Center or a table easel in the Art Center.

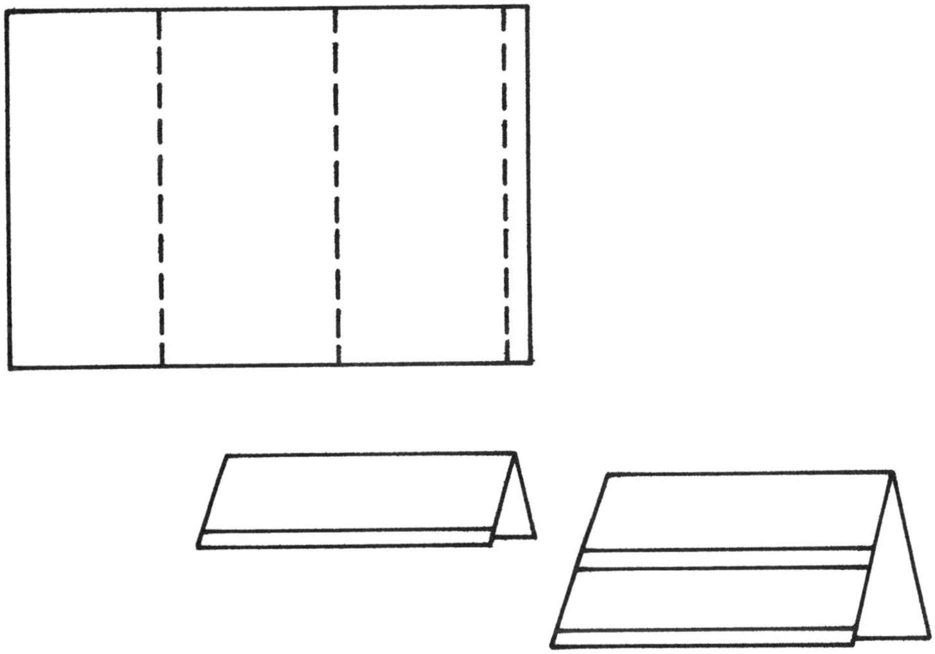

Cover a box with colorful vinyl adhesive to make a display stand. Cut a slit along the top surface of the box; then insert a chart into the slot. If you use this type of display, remember to leave blank space at the bottom of your charts so important information won't be covered up.

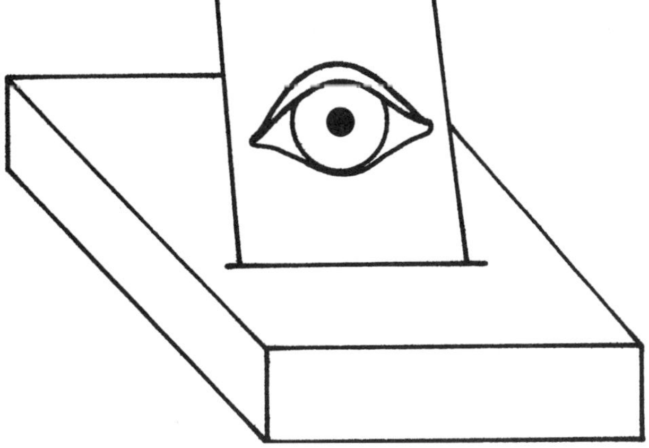

A "flip chart" makes a convenient rebus display. Punch holes along the top edges of charts; thread metal rings, heavy cord, or leather strips through the holes. Place your flip chart over a painting easel that can be easily moved from one area of the room to another.

Make small easels for single symbols or for short sequences of directions. Trim one end of a piece of posterboard to form a tab as show in the illustration below. Cut a slot in the other end of the strip, near the edge, then make folds by scoring the cardboard at desired intervals. After you have creased and folded the chart, insert the tab into the slot to form a freestanding easel.

These triangular stands can be folded for easy storage.

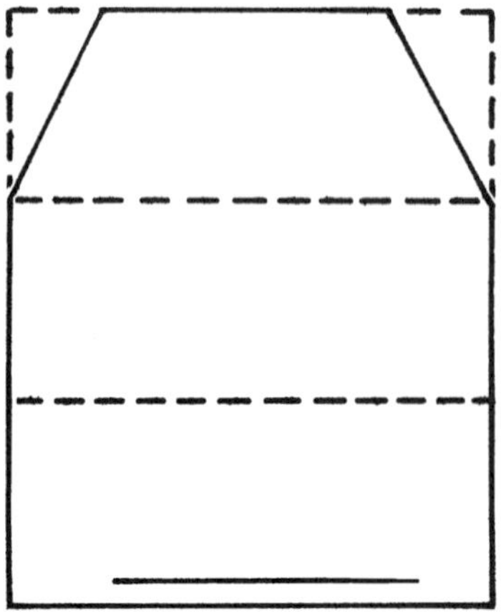

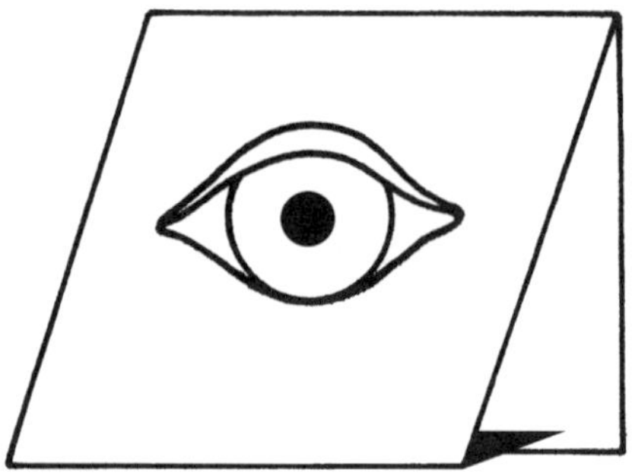

Storing Charts

Here are some suggestions for keeping charts in good condition and easy to locate.

The boxes in which posters are shipped make excellent vertical storage for charts; local school supply stores often give them away for free. Make different-colored tabs for charts from strips of oak tag and label them accordingly; you'll be able to easily identify and pull the charts you want from storage simply by glancing at the tabs.

Make a "rebus book" for each category of charts you're storing. Punch three holes in the sides of each chart and connect with metal rings so that you can add new charts. Children will enjoy looking through these homemade rebus "big books."

Copy individual steps of rebuses on separate 8 1/2" x 11" sheets of oak tag and store them in folders in a box or file drawer. Arrange each section of a particular rebus in correct order on posterboard or a bulletin board when you need it.

Tape individual cards together accordion-style. Fold and store on a bookshelf.

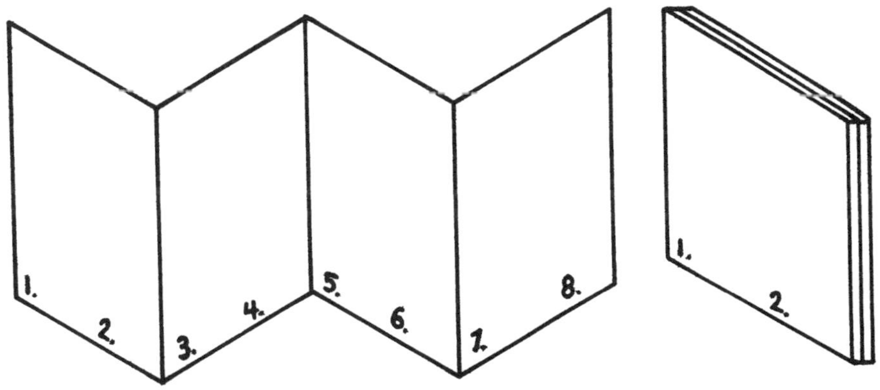

Duplicate individual steps you use repeatedly in many different rebuses (for instance, washing and drying hands, or hanging pictures to dry) and file away until you need them. Label each card with the title of the rebus or symbol chart and number where it belongs in sequence. When using the same steps in several rebus charts, use the same color of cardboard.

CHAPTER CHECKLIST

	Yes	No
1. Do I use basic symbol and rebus charts to help the children learn as independently as possible?		
2. Have I introduced the charts to children before they use them?		
3. Have I progressed from simple symbol and rebus charts to more complex charts?		
4. Have I included a second language with which the children are familiar if appropriate?		
5. Have I posted some self-help and grooming rebus charts around the room?		
6. Have I made sure to use manuscript printing on my rebus charts?		
7. Have I checked that the sequences of rebus charts are always left-to-right and top-to-bottom?		
8. Have I used a variety of natural tones for people and objects in my rebuses?		
9. Have I adapted my symbol or rebus charts to fit the needs of the children in my group?		
10. Have I made sure children can "read" the charts by following the drawings alone?		

General Symbols

1

Put on a smock.

2

Wash your hands.

General Symbols

Aa Bb Cc Dd Ee Ff

Gg Hh Ii Jj Kk Ll Mm

Nn Oo Pp Qq Rr Ss Tt

Uu Vv Ww Xx Yy Zz

1 2 3 4 5 6 7 8 9 10

Playing With Blocks

1

Choose the blocks.

2

Build with the blocks.

3

Put blocks away.

Planning Boards

A planning, or activity, board is one way to indirectly manage the number of children working in each center. Children refer to the planning board to see which activities they can choose, then attach their name tags to indicate the choices they have made.

Using a planning board encourages children to

- make decisions;
- stay with their choices and follow through on their actions;
- share and take turns;
- experience delayed gratification by sometimes having to wait for an area;
- negotiate and arbitrate;
- evaluate their learning by talking about where they played and what they did.

Setting Up Planning Boards

Planning boards can take one of two basic forms. For younger preschoolers, locate individual planning boards in each interest center. After some experience using the smaller planning boards, older preschoolers may be ready to use a single, centralized planning board.

A central planning board contains a representation of each individual interest center. Start by making name tags to use on your planning boards. Write each child's name in manuscript lettering on oak tag squares; laminate cards and punch holes in each one. Children can hang tags on corresponding hooks inserted into a pegboard. You can also use Velcro® on name tags *and* planning boards to make them especially easy for children to attach. Use stickers, animal pictures, or colored shapes on name tags so that children can match them to corresponding symbols in activity centers. Change symbols throughout the year for variety. Later, add children's last names to their tags.

Individual Planning Boards

Place individual planning boards made of peg board or poster board in each interest center. Each board should contain a picture of a typical activity for that center (for instance, using blocks to build a tower). Print the name of each center in manuscript lettering. Indicate how many children can play in a center at one time by the number of hooks Velcro® strips, or pockets in which children may place name tags.

Central Planning Board

Set up a central board this way:

Use the back of a bookcase or cabinet, a peg board divider, or a bulletin board to display activity choices.

Use colored tape to divide the central board into sections corresponding to the number of interest centers.

Place an interest-center marker— a photograph or drawing of children playing, or an appropriate picture of materials cut from a supply catalog— in each section of the board.

Cut squares from poster board and print the name of each center with different markers. Laminate or cover markers with adhesive paper.

Color-cue the central planning board markers to the identification markers in the individual centers.

Include enough "play spaces" (hooks, pockets, or Velcro® strips) in each interest center so that children have many choices.

Introducing Planning Boards

Before introducing either individual or central planning boards, make sure children know the names of the centers, where each is located, and what types of activities take place there. You may need to walk through the centers with the children each day, pointing out activities and materials.

Show children how to choose the interest center where they want to play by placing a name tag on the planning board.

Here are some other tips:

Start with individual interest-center planning boards, gradually introducing central planning boards over time.

Give children time to figure out the system and to assimilate the information.

Always include a symbolic representation to go with the printing on the name tags and on the center markers for the main planning board. Remember, your children may not be able to read, but they will soon recognize their names as well as the names of various interest centers.

Use large manuscript printing. Follow the letter patterns included on page 120. Children reproduce what they see, and some of them may be ready to print their names and a few simple words.

Share planning board procedures with parents.

Special Concerns When Using Planning Boards

To indicate that an interest center is closed

Remove hooks or print CLOSED on several cardboard circles. Punch holes in circles and hang them on the appropriate hooks.

Print CLOSED on the back of the name card for the interest center and turn it over.

If a central planning board is being used, place a CLOSED sign over that section of the planning board.

What to do with extra activity name cards

A divided household caddy provides storage space for unused cards, name tags, and extra pencils. Keep it near the central board.

When changing a center from one content area to another

Change the picture on the central planning board to correspond to its new use. For example, if the library is to become a puppet theater, remove the Library Center card and put up a planning board card picturing a puppet theater.

When an interest center is full

Some children will object, some will accept, and some will try to do something about the situation. One child might try to place one name on top of another. Another might move a name and replace it with his own. Still another might add a hook by taking it from another place.

Use positive limit-setting techniques to help the children learn how to handle this situation when it arises. Explain that if an interest center is full, a child may not play there until someone moves to a new center.

Have the children write their names or their "marks" on a waiting list near the center. This concrete reassurance that they will definitely have a turn makes waiting easier.

Teach children to negotiate. Ask them to help decide how they should be allowed to play in a center before moving on.

When a child chooses the same center over and over again

Regularly change the order in which children get to choose where they will play. That way, some choices will already be closed and the child will need to consider other options.

Make sure activities in other centers are truly interesting.

Consider simply allowing the child to continue playing in the same center. Try to observe why the child may be choosing one particular activity and use your observations to create related activities in other centers.

When a child moves from center to center with limited focus

Let the children help you establish a *minimum* amount of time everyone should remain at one center. Give children the option to *change* centers at the end of the period but *do not require them to do so.*

Praise time children spend on task. Use meaningful feedback to indicate why it might be worthwhile to stay with one activity for a period of time (For instance, *Karen worked really hard, and now she's made a whole castle!*).

Be sure the activities are interesting and within the appropriate developmental range.

When a child doesn't understand the interest-center procedure

Make a point of actually showing the child how to play in a center and move to another activity when necessary.

Let the child choose her activity first. Be available to help when the child shows a need for change.

Observe this child to figure out why she does not understand the procedure.

Planning and Evaluation

During group meetings or sharing circles, children can discuss the activities in the centers and what they will do. When evaluating, encourage the children to discuss where they have played and what they have done.

Chapter Checklist

		Yes	No
1.	Do I have a method of indirectly managing the number of children working in each center?		
2.	If I am using a planning board, does it fit the age and developmental stage of the children in my group: individual planning boards for threes and fours or children with no previous experience; central planning boards for older fours and fives?		
3.	Have I analyzed the number of play spaces in the room?		
4.	Are there one-and-a-half play spaces per child so that children have a variety of choices?		
5.	Did I make sure children know the names of the centers and that they have information about each center before introducing the planning board?		
6.	Did I introduce the planning board carefully?		
7.	Do I use the planning board on a regular basis?		
8.	Do I give individual assistance to children experiencing difficulty, or to new children?		
9.	Do I provide interesting and challenging activities in all learning centers so that one or two centers will not always be in high demand?		
10.	Have I provided a waiting list for some centers?		

Schedules

A good preschool schedule is the framework for effective indirect guidance in the classroom. The best schedule balances group time, individual time, and daily routines. It meets children's needs for quiet and active play periods according to the time of day. As children learn the sequence of daily tasks, you'll be free to interact with them in more meaningful ways.

Evaluating Your Schedule

One way to evaluate whether your schedule is effective is by listening to children describe it to you, their parents, or visitors. If children consistently say, for instance, *First we have a snack, next we wash up, and then we sing songs*, they probably have a good grasp of daily routines.

Here is an example of a schedule using picture cues.

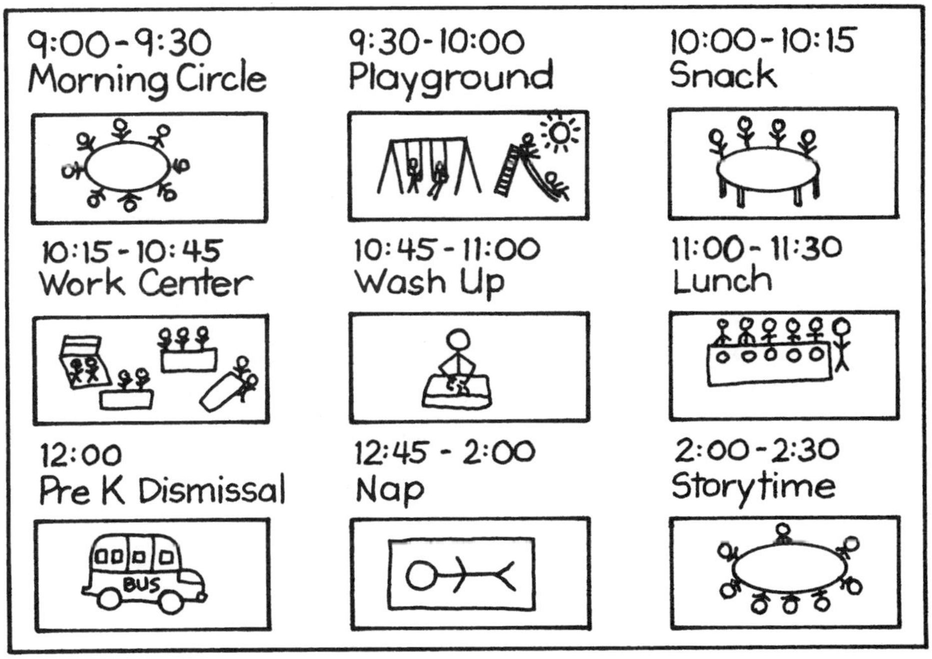

If you work with two- and three-year-old children, use photographs to make the schedule more concrete. Photograph the children during important regular activities like morning arrival, snack, interest centers, outdoor centers, lunch time, and nap time (or use photos you took in previous years). Mount the photographs in sequence starting at the top.

You may want to post each photograph on a separate, laminated card and let children help you sequence them during sharing circle before each day begins. Either way, discuss the chart with children before you display it.

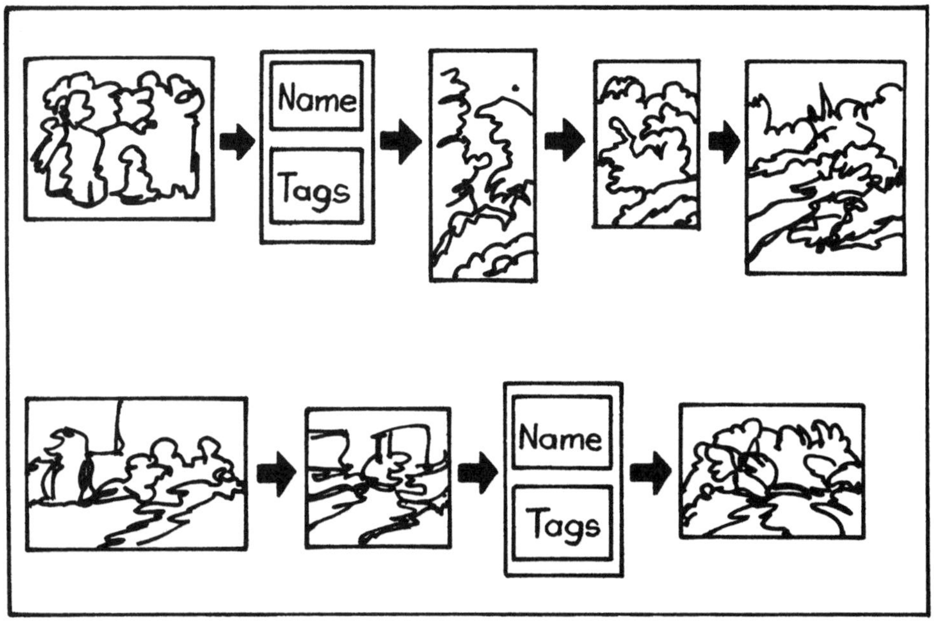

Alert other staff members to your schedule so that everyone can plan accordingly for special events and know where to find you in emergencies.

During the first few weeks of school, follow the schedule very carefully. Once you firmly establish the routine, you can make changes if necessary. For example, on a day that threatens rain, you might say, *Today we are going outside first because it looks like it might rain. We might not be able to go outside later. There will be time to play in the interest centers before lunch.* This simple explanation lets children know the reason for the change and reassures them that they are not going to miss an activity they might be anticipating.

Using a Schedule

Carefully plan routines like arrivals and departures, meals, rest periods, and toileting. Using routine time effectively can influence how smoothly each day proceeds. Chapter 8 provides indirect-guidance ideas to use during routines.

Space and Time Requirements

When creating your schedule, don't forget to consider the space and time requirements of other classes using the same facility. Combine children of various age groups if such combinations follow state licensing standards. In cases when children arrive and leave on a staggered schedule, try combining groups at the beginning and end of the day. Quiet, self-directed activities work well for these occasions.

Balanced Activities

Alternate active and quiet times in your schedule. For example, you might want to consider planning story time to follow outdoor play periods.

Also try to alternate group time with periods of individual play. This will provide children with variety and help them better tolerate the necessary constraints of group meetings.

Plan for large group times to be short. Make sure to allow sufficient time for interest center activities so all children have an opportunity to finish their activities. Knowing that they have reasonable times to finish tasks will help children become more involved in activities from the outset.

Children have different learning styles. Some children watch for a long time before becoming deeply involved in an activity. Other children dive right in and finish quickly, taking part in several activities during one interest-center period. As a result, you may want to limit how often children rotate from centers without completely discouraging changes.

To help children develop cooperative learning skills, plan some large-group activities that involve all or most of the class. If there is more than one adult in the classroom, try to schedule time in small groups. Children will have more opportunities to participate, spend much less time waiting, and receive more individualized teaching.

Consider using transitional activities to help children move more easily from one activity to another. Transitional activities usually take the form of finger plays, songs, or quick games. Chapter 9 gives ideas for transitional activities based on indirect-guidance techniques.

Finally, don't forget to take into account for the needs and availability of staff members during the day. Everyone needs time to plan, attend meetings, and participate in workshops.

Sample Schedules

The schedule you develop should meet the needs of children, parents, *and* staff. Here are some examples of schedules that work well in various circumstances; feel free to adapt them accordingly.

A Sample Toddler Schedule

7:30 – 8:00	Arrival — Self-selected activities and guided exploration
8:00 – 8:35	Clean up and transition to breakfast/snack
8:35 – 9:50	Self-selected activities and guided exploration
9:50 – 10:00	Clean up and transition to outdoors
10:00 – 11:00	Outdoor centers and activities
11:00 – 11:05	Transition to inside
11:05 – 11:15	Quiet guided exploration
11:15 – 11:45	Transition to and preparation for lunch; lunch
11:45 – 12:00	Nap/rest preparation (tooth brushing, toileting, diapering)
12:00 – 2:30	Nap/rest
1:00 – 2:30	Quiet activities for those awake; additional centers open as more children wake up
2:30 – 2:50	Transition/preparation for snack; snack
2:50 – 2:55	Transition to outdoor centers
2:55 – 3:45	Outdoor centers and activities
3:45 – 3:50	Transition to inside
3:50 – 5:30	Self-selected activities and guided exploration
5:30	Center Closed

A Sample Schedule for Threes and Fours

7:00 – 8:00	Arrival and quiet activities
8:00 – 8:05	Clean up
8:05 – 8:10	Prepare for breakfast
8:10 – 8:30	Breakfast
8:30 – 8:40	Good morning group activity
8:40 – 9:45	Indoor learning centers
9:45 – 9:55	Clean up
9:55 – 10:00	Prepare for snack
10:00 – 10:10	Snack
10:10 – 10:15	Transition to outdoors
10:15 – 11:10	Outdoor learning center
11:10 – 11:15	Transition to indoors
11:15 – 11:25	Language arts activity (children look at books individually or in pairs or trios)
11:25 – 11:35	Preparation for lunch
11:35 – 12:00	Lunch
12:00 – 2:00	Nap/rest
1:00 – 2:00	Quiet activities for those awake
2:00 – 2:30	Put cots away; prepare for snack; snack
2:30 – 2:40	Music/movement group activity
2:40 – 3:45	Indoor learning centers
3:45 – 3:55	Clean up
3:55 – 4:00	Transition to outdoors
4:00 – 4:55	Outdoor learning centers
4:55 – 5:00	Transition to indoors
5:00 - 6:00	Quiet activities

CHAPTER CHECKLIST

	Yes	No
1. Do I have a current schedule posted in my classroom?		
2. Is the schedule represented in sequenced pictorial form so children can "read" it?		
3. Have I planned for routines like meal times, rest, and toileting?		
4. Are active times balanced with quieter times?		
5. Have I planned for quiet time before lunch?		
6. Are child-directed activities alternated with teacher-directed times?		
7. Have I scheduled transitional activities to assist children through the day's routines?		
8. Are large group periods of appropriate length for my age group?		
9. Have I tried to arrange for most group activities to take place in small groups rather than in one large one?		
10. Are the scheduling needs of other classes and the needs and availability of other staff members taken into consideration in this schedule?		

Routines

Routines are a necessary part of the daily schedule in any early childhood program. Routines that lend themselves to indirect-guidance techniques include

- arrival and departure
- eating (snacks and meals)
- sleeping and resting
- toileting
- grooming

As part of the daily schedule, use self-directed activities to help children learn to handle routines.

Arrival and Departure

Arrival and departure times offer an opportunity for children to make choices about how they will begin and end each day.

Provide a place near the door where children can keep their belongings and store things to take home. Mark each child's space with a name card and a predesignated individual symbol. Mark each coat hook in the same way. Provide a place for coats, extra clothes, and backpacks.

Arrival and departure times also afford opportunities for you to communicate with parents, and vice-versa.

Here are some suggestions:

Provide a special bulletin board for parents that includes information about topics you're studying in class, plus a pocket filled with copies of songs, finger plays, and stories children have learned. Display a *What We Need* poster asking for items you can use for class projects. Clearly mark the date when you will need materials and provide a box or basket under the poster for collecting items.

Post a *Where Did You Play Today?* chart near the entry door. Print the names of the interest centers horizontally across the top and children's names down the side. Each day, children can help you fill in the chart before they go home. Add a new page to the chart each week so that it becomes a cumulative record.

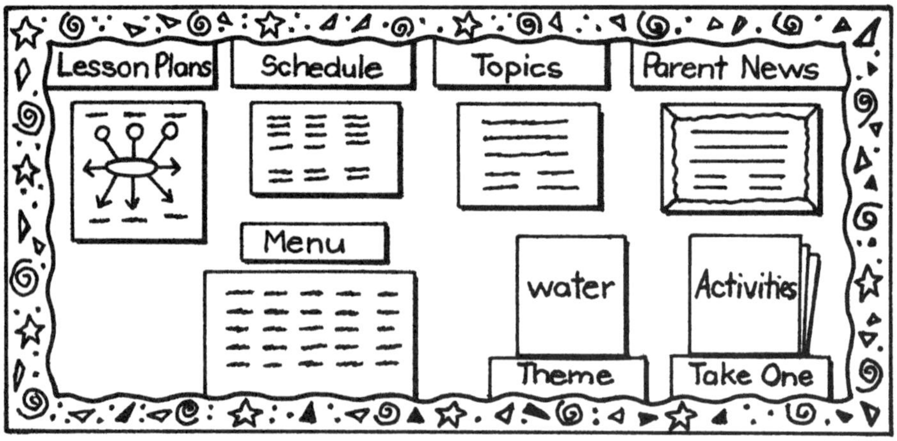

Social Skills at Meal Times

Snacks or meals provide many opportunities for indirect guidance. Children will be practicing social behaviors like taking turns and engaging in conversation. Children particularly enjoy eating food that they have prepared using the rebus charts.

Here are other mealtime suggestions:

Make placemats that show where plates, glasses, and utensils belong.

Reserve this time to teach some special skill indirectly. For example, mealtime conversation may be in a second language, especially if many children know or frequently hear that language.

Post a weekly menu that includes pictures of foods children will eat on that particular day.

Use a "Helpers' Chart" to improve self-direction during eating times, as well as for other routines. The chart shows the names of children who are helpers for the day. Jobs might include setting the tables, scraping plates, or sweeping the floor. Use real pictures or photographs of the children themselves. Helpers charts for older preschoolers can include symbols and simple words.

Self-Help at Rest Time

Children frequently have difficulty settling down for rest periods. If children participate in scheduling this time, they may accept it more readily.

Help children decide the length of time for rests or naps. Offer acceptable choices that fit into the requirements of the program and any state licensing standards. With indirect guidance, children can decide which times they wish to rest on their cots or mats, how long they can look at books or play quietly, and how and what they should do when rest time is over.

Help children prepare for rest periods by using special cot sheets that are easy for children to change themselves.

Here's how to make cot sheets:

1. Cut the fabric to fit cot measurements, plus two inches on each side to provide for 1" double hems.

2. Turn over the corners at a right angle and stitch them down.

3. Sew elastic to the outside of the triangles formed at two corners.

4. Fasten the other two ends with strips of fabric that children can snap, button, or tie.

Mark cots with each child's name and symbol. Display the children's artwork from the ceiling and walls in the rest area. Place children's cots under their art so they'll know where to find their rest spaces. The artwork also provides something children can focus on while resting.

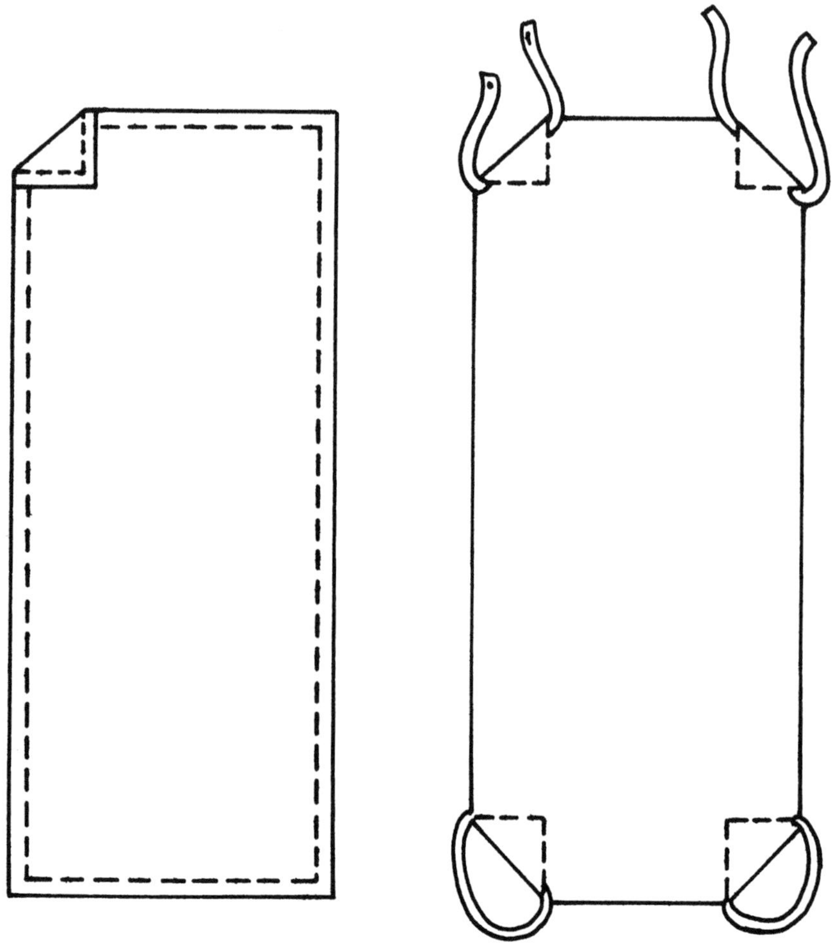

Grooming Time

Rebus charts are very effective indirect-guidance techniques for grooming time. Charts can show how to wash and dry hands, brush teeth, and use tissues. Use disposable paper cups marked with names and symbols to store toothbrushes. (If your routine differs from the routine described, alter the chart to reflect your needs.)

Because children should wash their hands after they blow their noses, add a portion of the hand-washing rebus to the nose blowing chart. Rebuses should be placed next to the tissue box and close to a plastic-lined, covered container.

Safety Routines

Regularly practice fire drills to help children exit the building quickly and in an orderly fashion. To remind children of this important information, mark the appropriate exit at child level with an exit sign and display a fire drill rebus.

Picture cues are also helpful for adults. Post a Red Cross sign showing the location of first-aid supplies in your room.

CHAPTER CHECKLIST

	Yes	No
1. Have I provided a place near the door where children can store their personal belongings?		
2. Have I marked each child's personal storage area with his or her name and symbol?		
3. Am I using the area near the door as a way to communicate with parents?		
4. Am I using indirect guidance during mealtimes to encourage independence and self-direction?		
5. Am I using indirect guidance during nap time to encourage independence and self-direction?		
6. Have I provided rebus charts for such activities as hand washing, tooth brushing, and nose blowing?		
7. Have I marked exits and displayed a fire drill rebus at children's eye level?		
8. Have I provided picture cues for adults as well as for children?		

Flossing Teeth

1

Cut off a long piece of floss.

2

Wrap floss around fingers.

Flossing Teeth

3

Run floss between teeth.

4

Throw floss in trash.

Brushing Teeth

1

Wet your toothbrush.

2

Put toothpaste on your toothbrush.

3

Brush your teeth.

Brushing Teeth

4

Rinse your toothbrush.

5

Rinse your mouth.

6

Return your toothbrush to your cup.

Washing Hands

1

Wet hands.

2

Add soap.

Washing Hands

3

Rinse your hands.

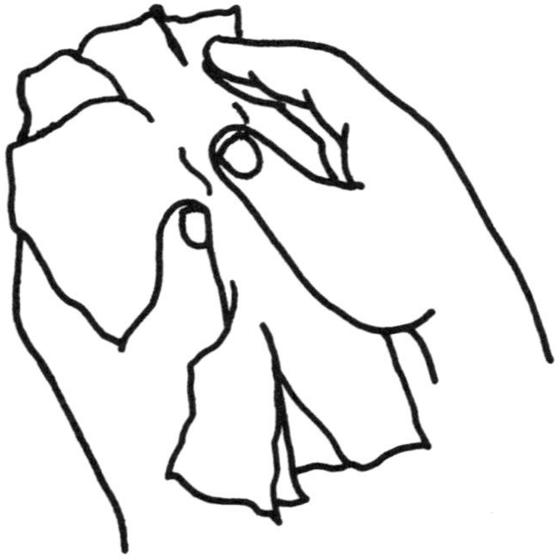

4

Dry your hands with a paper towel.

5

Toss the paper towel in the trash.

Using Tissues

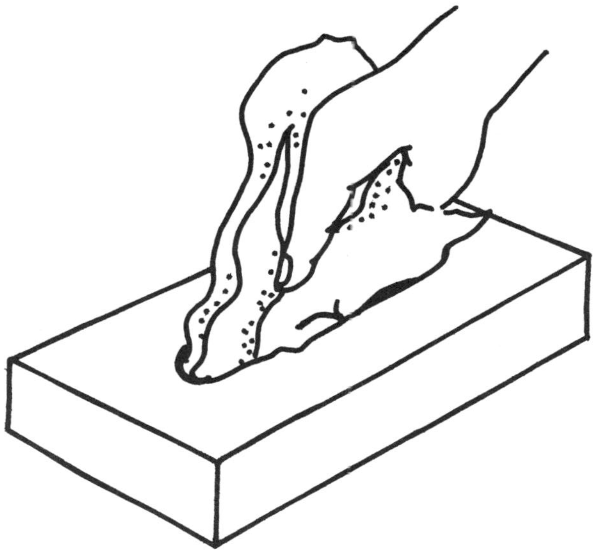

1

Take a tissue.

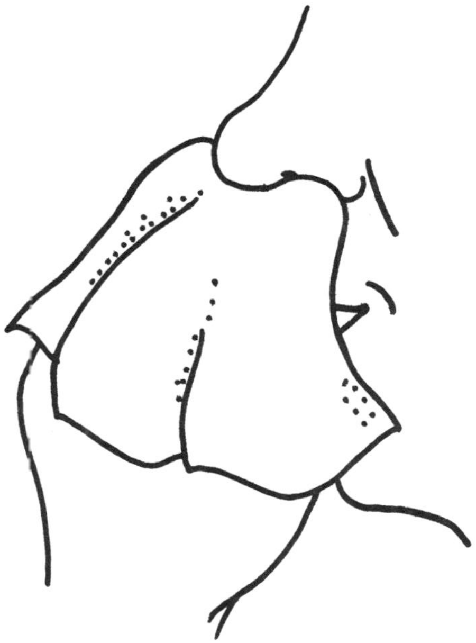

2

Use the tissue.

3

Toss the tissue in the trash.

Toileting

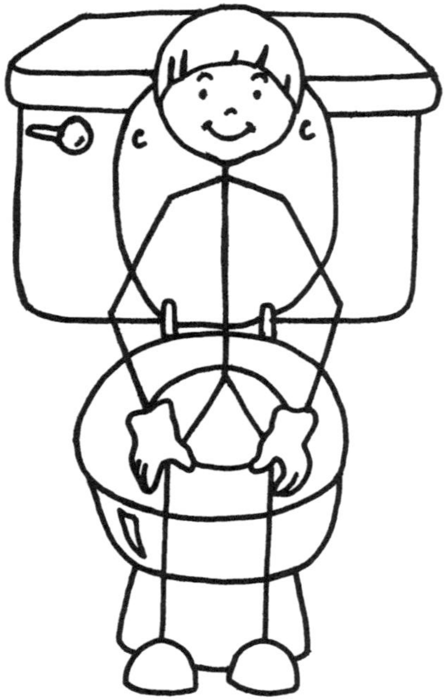

1

Use the toilet.

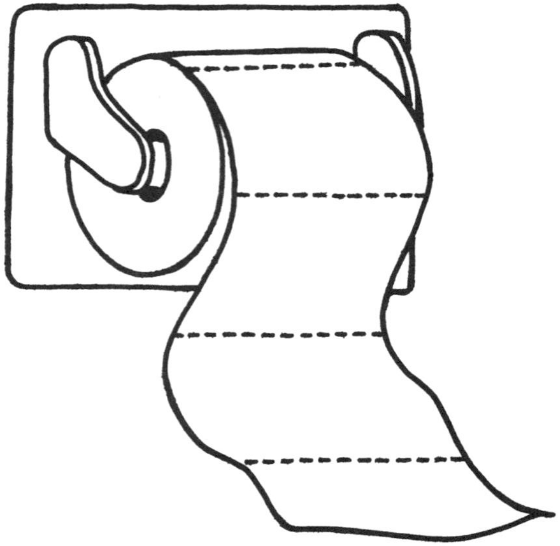

2

Wipe with toilet tissue.

Toileting

3

Throw the toilet tissue in the toilet.

4

Flush the toilet.

8

Setting Limits

An important part of teaching young children is meeting their physical needs for food, sleep, clothing, exercise, and protection from harm. But you also provide many of children's psychological and emotional needs for love, acceptance, and respect. The way you treat children will help them believe that they are worthwhile individuals.

There's no way to completely avoid the conflicts and behavior problems that are part of being human. Children *want* guidelines and limits. When they take part in defining those limits, they tend to claim ownership for their behavior much more readily than if guidelines are dictated by adults only. Understanding what's expected of them also helps children feel more secure and able to take the risks so important to learning.

Planning for Individual Differences

Teaching situations vary; each group of children has its own characteristics. Think of last year's class. No doubt, in spite of a wide range of differences between individuals, that class had a different overall *tone* than this year's. Every time you get ready to welcome a new group of children, you're prepared to be a little surprised by how they function as a whole and to make changes and adjustments as the year progresses.

Your approach to setting limits may depend on:

- stages of maturation and development;
- ages of children;
- different cultures;
- consideration of the rights of other children and adults;
- health and safety;
- the activities you're considering.

When to Set Limits

To determine whether a child's behavior is out-of-bounds, ask yourself the following questions:

- Is the behavior unsafe to the child or to others? Is the behavior unhealthy? (Remember that children need to take "safe" risks to grow and develop.)
- Is the behavior resulting in destruction of property?
- Is the behavior showing disrespect for other children or adults?
- Is the behavior enabling a child to avoid responsibility?

If the answer to any of those questions is *yes,* then you probably need to set limits for the child or situation. Remember, *ignoring* inappropriate behavior is one of the most powerful and effective ways to change it and may be the appropriate action to take initially. Often, when children realize they are not going to be rewarded for inappropriate behaviors, they'll find healthier ways to get feedback.

Enforcing Limits

Limits are effective only if they are consistently enforced and individualized for the child or situation. Discipline is most useful when you take into account the child's age, stage of development, cultural background, personality, and any stressful situations he or she is facing, such as a divorce.

Consider these guidelines when enforcing limits:

Children are responsible for their own behavior.

Children are more responsive to adults' requests when they believe that their feelings have been heard and understood. Active listening is one of your most powerful disciplinary tools. Reflect children's feelings back to them, THEN use a limit-setting technique. For example, if a child drops her coat on the floor instead of putting it in her cubby, say, *You are in such a hurry that you didn't put your coat away.* Then use one of the techniques described below.

Give children an opportunity to correct their own actions. Provide enough information so that children have options for making good choices: *You dropped your coat on the floor. Coats belong in cubbies.*

Let children know how you feel about a behavior and what its effects might be: *When I see your coat on the floor, I worry that someone might trip over it.*

Whenever possible, give choices between acceptable alternatives: *You may put your coat away by yourself, or I can help you.*

Let children know there are consequences to certain behaviors, but try to state these effects in positive terms: *When you have put your coat away, you can join us in sharing circle.*

When a child tests limits, be firm. Use a neutral tone of voice and facial expression. Avoid power struggles.

Give positive feedback for appropriate behaviors.

CHAPTER CHECKLIST

	Yes	No
1. Have I implemented indirect-guidance techniques to eliminate most inappropriate behaviors?		
2. When setting limits, do I consider the children's ages, developmental stages, cultural backgrounds, and individual personalities?		
3. When deciding if a behavior is exceeding limits, do I consider safety, responsibility, respect, and protection of property?		
4. Do I ignore inappropriate behavior when possible?		
5. Do I use positive limit-setting techniques when limits are being exceeded?		
6. Do I start by allowing the child to take responsibility for his or her own behavior, then progress to techniques that require more responsibility for guiding the child's behavior?		
7. Do I name the child's feelings before I use a limit-setting technique?		

TRANSITIONAL ACTIVITIES

9

Transitions are all those times when children are moving from one activity (or setting) to another. The first transition is when children arrive at school. Other transitions occur as your children choose activities, clean up after center time, or gather for group time.

Transitions can be confusing. Children are usually trying to complete activities, clean up, begin new activities, or move to another part of the classroom. Sometimes, long periods of waiting are a part of making transitions, and waiting is especially difficult for young children. Teachers end up spending extra time and energy trying to control their behavior.

Fortunately, you can use transition time for purposeful learning activities. Planning activities that help children move from one time block to the next helps the schedule flow much more smoothly.

Transitions From Home to School

The first transition of the day is from home to school. The way children and adults handle separating can set the tone for the rest of the day, especially for toddlers and children who are new to your program.

Older preschoolers may benefit from a simple activity that will help them gradually get back into the school frame of mind. For example, place a box labeled *attendance* on a shelf or small table near the door. Before children arrive, arrange individual name cards on a table or counter. As children arrive, encourage them to locate their name cards and place them in the box. Later in the year, add last names to cards.

Or string a clothesline across the back of a shelf or divider. As children come in, they can attach their name cards to the line with clothespins.

Cleanup

Give children some warning that clean-up time is approaching so they can finish whatever they are doing. Since preschoolers can't yet tell time, quietly tell children at each interest center, *It is almost time for cleanup. You have some time left to play, and then we will clean up so that we can have our group time*. Remind them to listen for a special clean-up signal.

Songs are especially helpful in helping young children know when it's time to clean up. Introduce some clean-up songs to children early in the year; make sure you use them on a regular basis so children come to recognize them as signals for this activity. Make sure to include some clean-up songs in any folders you prepare for substitutes.

Clean-Up Songs

Oh, Do You Know What Time It Is?

(To the tune of *Do You Know the Muffin Man?)*

Oh, do you know what time it is?
What time it is, what time it is?
Oh, do you know what time it is?
It's almost clean-up time.

A Helper I Will Be

(To the tune of *The Farmer in the Dell)*

A helper I will be,
A helper I will be.
Hi ho the dairy-o,
A helper I will be.
I'll put the blocks away,
I'll put the blocks away.
Hi ho the dairy-o,
I'll put the blocks away.

Before and After Group Time

Transition activities as children leave and enter group activities could include an attention-getter to help gather and settle the children, a quieting activity, and a dismissal activity when group time is over. Create predictable and manageable movements from one activity time to another.

Consider the following when planning transitional group activities:

Children's physical skills. Do children possess the motor skills a particular activity requires? Remember that young preschoolers need to use large hand movements or simple body movements.

Children's language skills. Look for activities that involve lots of repetition. Vocabulary should also be appropriate for the age group.

Classroom themes. If you tie transitional activities to the theme used for group activities, there will be a smoother flow into and out of group time.

Use some of these songs for gathering and settling down:

Come Over Here

(Tune: *Mary Had a Little Lamb*)

Come over here and sit right down,
sit right down, sit right down.
Come over here and sit right down,
We're going to be together.

Coming to the Circle

(Set to any companionable tune)

Friends, friends, come right here;
Friends, friends, come right here;
Friends, friends, come right here;
It's time to have our circle!
Jeremy, Jeremy, come right here;
Susie, Susie, come right here;
Sharon and Billie, come right here;
It's time to have our circle!

Quieting Activities

Here are some suggestions that help children get ready to pay attention, focus, or calm down before an activity.

Grandma's Glasses

These are Grandma's glasses,
 (Make circles with the thumbs and forefingers)
This is Grandma's hat,
 (Make round hat with hands)
This is the way she folds her hands.
 (Place one hand on top of another)
And puts them in her lap.
 (Put hands in lap)
Here are Grandpa's glasses,
 (Make glasses)
Here is Grandpa's hat.
 (Make pointed hat)
This is the way he folds his arms
 (Fold arms)
And sits like that.

Roll Them and Roll Them
Roll them and roll them and give a little clap.
Roll them and roll them and put them in your lap.

Touch Exercise
Il touch my hair, my lips, my eyes.
(Do motions as you say words)
I'll sit up straight, and then I'll rise.
I'll touch my eyes, my nose, my chin,
Then quietly sit down again.

Clap Your Hands
Clap your hands, clap your hands,
(Do motions as you say words)
Clap them just like me.
Touch your shoulders, touch your shoulders,
Touch them just like me.
Tap your knees, tap your knees,
Tap them just like me.
Shake your head, shake your head.
Shake it just like me.
Clap your hands, clap your hands,
Now let them quiet be.

Ten Little Fingers
I have ten little fingers and they all belong to me.
I can make them do things. Would you like to see?
I can make them jump high, I can make them jump low.
Or I can fold them together and hold them just so.

You can also make up poems and finger plays that are related to the theme you're exploring. Here is a poem to quiet children before hearing a story about a picnic.

After a Picnic
After a picnic
All day in the park,
It's time to go home,
It's getting dark.
I get ready for bed,
I lie down for sleep.
I don't make a sound,
Not even a peep.

Dismissing Activities

Link some aspect of the activity that's concluding with the next activity in the schedule. For example, if you're reading a story about shoes, say *All children wearing tennis shoes can wash their hands for lunch.* If you have just finished sampling different kinds of fruit, ask children to give an example of their favorite fruit before they leave the group.

Also, try using stuffed animals or puppets to help ease transitions. For instance, you could say, *When the puppy kisses your nose, you will be ready to put your jacket on.*

Use a planning board to help children select and move to interest centers. For more information, see Chapter 5.

Transitions to Outdoors

How you move your group of children to the outdoor play area will depend on how many adults are available to supervise and how far away the outdoor space is. If your classroom exits directly out onto the playground area and there are two adults in the room, you can move children by twos or threes to their cubbies (if they need jackets) and then to the door. One adult is indoors, using a transitional activity to cue children when it is their turn to go outside, and one adult is outdoors to supervise the other children.

If your classroom is far from the outdoor area, and there are two adults with the group, you may want to split the group in half.

If you are the only adult, you and the children should move outdoors together. Avoid having children line up at the door for a long period of time. Instead, try singing a song to cue the behavior you expect. One of our favorites follows:

Let's walk to our cubbies
And put on our coats;
Let's walk to our cubbies
And put on our coats;
Let's walk to our cubbies
And put on our coats;
It's time to go outside and play.
Let's tiptoe to the door
All together;
Let's tiptoe to the door
All together;
Let's tiptoe to the door
All together;
Now we can go outside and play!

Transition to Nap or Rest Times

When children are still eating lunch, begin to dim the classroom lights and play soothing music. As the children finish lunch and scrape their plates, help them move to the sink to brush their teeth. Remind them to use the toilet before getting on their cots or mats and to retrieve their nap toys (soft animals or dolls) and blankets from their cubbies before they lie down on their cots.

By now, the room is dim as the music continues to play. Try not to engage in conversation at this time. One adult can finish wiping off the lunch tables while another adult supervises the children on their cots. If you're teaching by yourself, let the final cleaning of tables and floors wait until the children are quieted and on their cots.

Children who do not fall asleep should be allowed to engage in quiet activities, like looking at books and coloring by themselves, after a brief rest period.

CHAPTER CHECKLIST

		Yes	No
1.	Have I included transition activities throughout my daily schedule?		
2.	Do I avoid having the children in my group wait for long periods of time?		
3.	Do I avoid activities that require children to sit still, wait, and be quiet?		
4.	Do I plan transitional activities that reinforce learning?		
5.	Are my transitional activities enjoyable and fun for the children?		
6.	Have I planned ways to help children make a smooth transition from home to school?		
7.	Do I give warnings before transitions?		
8.	Do I use songs and finger plays to guide children's behavior rather than direct commands?		
9.	When planning transitional activities, have I taken into consideration children's physical skills?		
10.	When planning transitional activities, have I taken into consideration children's language skills?		

10

Group Times

Group experiences are important parts of the daily routine in any early childhood setting.

These experiences might include the following:

- gathering together to start or end the day;
- planning and evaluating daily activities;
- hands-on activities related to a specific school or classroom theme;
- music and movement activities;
- story or language arts activities;
- cooking;
- meeting classroom visitors.

Take into consideration the age and developmental levels of your children when making decisions about group time. Because group activities often require children to listen and sit still, group experiences for infants or toddlers should be limited or eliminated altogether.

If you teach toddlers, plan and prepare materials for guided exploration which can take place during learning center periods. Sit on the floor and interact with children as they come to you. Once they lose interest in an activity, children should feel free to move to another activity. You may decide at that point to put the activity away until later.

If you teach preschool, plan short group times that are fun and engaging. Children should always have alternative choices for solo activities like looking at books in the library or playing with puzzles at the manipulatives table. If most of the children choose activities other than group time, you probably need to reevaluate your planning. Maybe your children aren't developmentally ready for working in large groups over extended periods, or perhaps you need to plan more interesting hands-on activities for group time.

Planning Group Activities

When selecting activities, take into consideration the age levels and abilities of your children. Use their interests as the basis for planning group activities. Involve as many of the five senses as possible in experiments and explorations. Use props to maintain focus and make activities as interactive as possible. For instance, when planning a group cooking experience, include steps children can participate in. The cooking rebuses at the end of Chapter 2 encourage children's participation.

Read to infants and young toddlers individually or in pairs. Read to older toddlers and threes and fours in small groups during learning center time. Introduce group stories to older fours and fives, but remember to allow them to choose a different activity if they desire. Look for stories that contain patterns, rhymes, and refrains so children can "read" them with you. Plan questions to ask either before or after the story. For a smooth transition, make any extended learning activities fit the story.

Be supportive of children as they interact or respond to questions. Ask questions that have many answers. Some teachers encourage children to select friends to help them when they can't think of an answer.

MANAGING LARGE GROUPS

Usually, small-group activities are more beneficial for young children than larger meetings. But some periods of large-group interaction may be necessary because of staff limitations or the nature of certain activities. Working in larger groups does teach children that they must sometimes adapt their behavior to different situations and that choices are occasionally limited. Prepare an area of the room for large-group gatherings. Sometimes, with a little coaching, children can conduct their own group activities. You may have to get the group started on a story, a musical activity, or a sharing time, but you can then relinquish control to the children and become part of the group yourself.

USE SYMBOLS

Group children by using cut-outs of animals, shapes, or different colored stars. Children match the symbol you give them with symbols they find in specific center areas.

During group meetings, use basic eye, hand, ear, and nose symbols discussed in Chapter 4 to gain children's attention, give directions, and smooth transitions. An eye and a mouth could alert the children to look first and then talk. A question mark reminds children to think of possible solutions.

Group by Area

Another way to group children is to designate particular areas by name; for example, *the circle area, the triangle area,* and *the square area.* Mobiles could also mark locations for group meetings. Children match their name tag designs with markers to find where they should go for an activity. To rotate groups, change name tag symbols periodically.

Singing and Signing

Young children can learn simple hand movements from sign language. Plan a visit from a person who uses sign language. Tell the visitor the signs that the children know, so that they can show how well they communicate this way. Use rebus stories and songs during small-or large-group story and music experiences. Many songs can be adapted for rebus charts. Try to limit the size of the group to five or six children during such activities so that everyone can see the singing charts.

STRATEGIES FOR GROUP MUSIC

Introduce some rhythm instruments and show children how to hold and play each one. Then place instruments in the music center along with the appropriate symbols. After children become familiar with rhythm instruments, introduce sounds and rhythms of different cultures; for instance, with a Chilean *rainstick* or a Mexican *guiro*.

Show drawings of rhythm instruments included at the end of this chapter. Ask children to play an instrument each time it's pictured. Keep the sequences simple, using only two or three instruments.

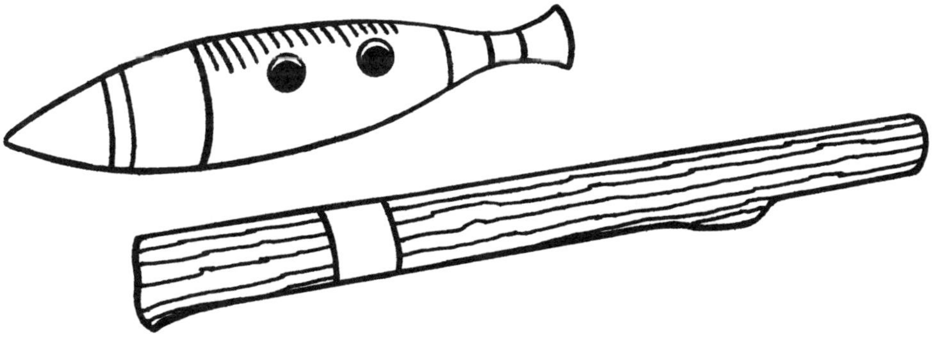

Use patterns for clapping out rhythms, playing instruments, or engaging children in guessing games. These activities work best with small groups of six or fewer children.

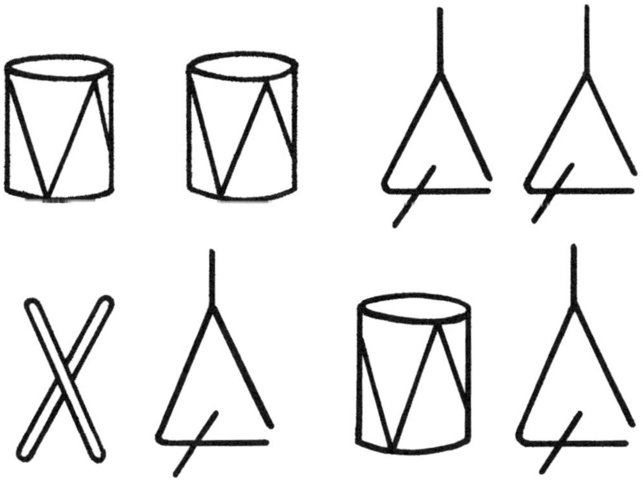

Arrange several copies of hand and foot patterns on a chart in sequence to show rhythmic patterns, such as $\frac{4}{4}$ time. Instruct the children to clap one time for each hand symbol and stamp one of their feet once for each foot symbol.

GROUP COOKING

Use the cooking rebuses at the end of Chapter 2 for small and large group experiences. After you have introduced the process to the group, try planning simple cooking activities for an interest center. This works best during snack time, when children can follow the rebus chart to prepare basic foods.

Cooking lessons are particularly effective in small groups. Plan the activity over several days and keep a record of participants so that each child has a chance to cook.

CHAPTER CHECKLIST

		Yes	No
1.	Do I plan my group times carefully?		
2.	Do I plan activities that are broad enough to fit the range of abilities of children in my class?		
3.	Am I making group activities interactive?		
4.	Do I support the children's interactions and responses during group time?		
5.	Do I divide my children into smaller groups when appropriate?		
6.	Have I tried using different symbols to divide children into groups?		
7.	Have I carefully introduced musical instruments to children?		
8.	Have I included instruments of other cultures?		
9.	Have I used music rebus charts?		
10.	Have I planned cooking activities which involve children in the preparation process?		

Rhythm Instruments

Drum

Maracas

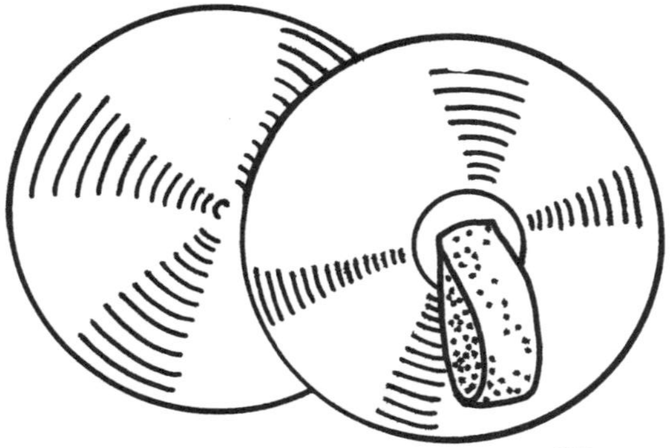

Cymbals

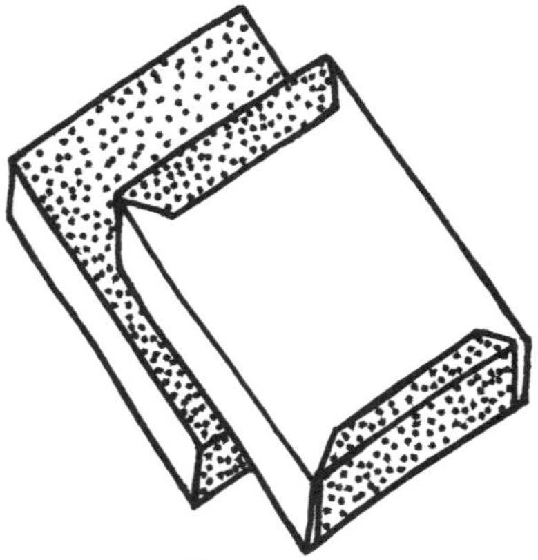

Sand Blocks

Rhythm Instruments

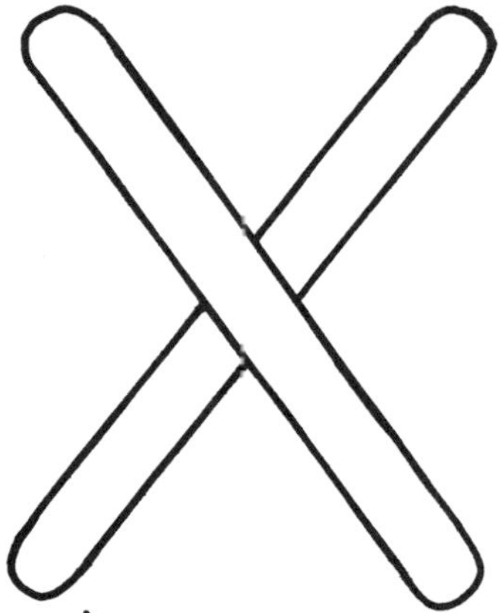

Rhythm Sticks

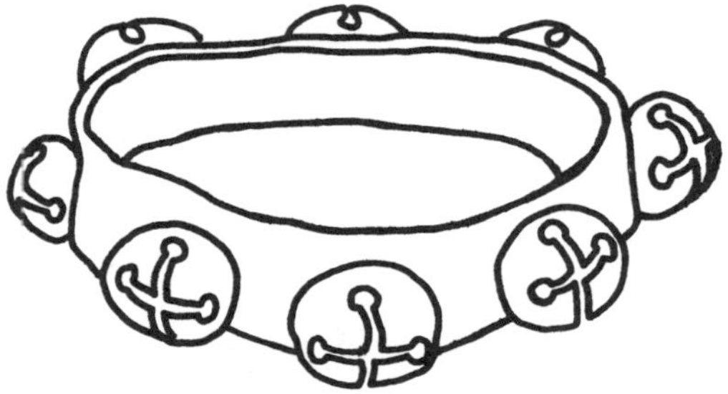

Bells

Triangle

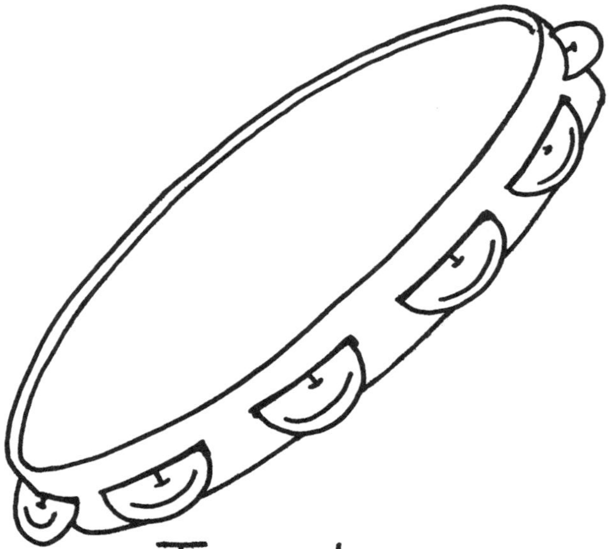

Tambourine

TEACHER NOTES

Teacher Notes

TEACHER NOTES